Zombie Preparedness

A Guide to Surviving the Zombie Apocalypse

Volume I

James C. Sanders

Copyright © 2013 James C. Sanders

All rights reserved.

ISBN: 1483976262
ISBN-13: 978-1483976266

CONTENTS

1	Predicting Outbreaks	7
2	Psychology of Zombie Survival	19
3	Survival Planning	31
4	Zombie Survival Actions	41
5	Medical	49
6	Water Procurement	75
7	Food Procurement	83
8	Zombie Combat	107
9	Survival Movement in Zombie Infested Areas	121
10	Long Term Survival Solutions	131
	Appendix A Undead Will	139
	Appendix B Goal Setting	144
	Appendix C Adapted Standardized Hand Signals for Close Range Engagement (C.R.E.)	148

DEADICATION

To all the living preparing to survive the undead.

ACKNOWLEDGMENTS

I would like to express the deepest appreciation to
the United States Air Force for my training,
the United States Army for the field guide so heavily represented in this book,
freegrunge.com for the zombie clipart,
family, friends, and loved ones who tolerate my incessant focus on the undead,
and the government and private sources of insight to, and knowledge of,
the secretive world of zombie outbreaks.

1 – PREDICTING OUTBREAKS

Zombies are real.

Many civilizations throughout recorded history experienced or predicted zombie outbreaks. The proof is in their religious and historical text.

1300-1000 BC The Epic of Gilgamesh
I will raise up the dead and they will eat the living. And the dead will outnumber the living.

518-516 BC Holy Bible
Zechariah 14:12 & 13
And the LORD will send a plague on all the nations that fought against Jerusalem. Their people will become like walking corpses, their flesh rotting away. Their eyes will rot in their sockets, and their tongues will rot in their mouths. On that day they will be terrified, stricken by the LORD with great panic. They will fight their neighbors hand to hand.

609-632 AD Qur'an
Surat al-Qamar: 6-8

Turn away from them then. On the Day the Summoner summons them to something unspeakably terrible, they will emerge from their graves with downcast eyes, like swarming locusts, necks outstretched, eyes transfixed, rushing headlong to the Summoner. The disbelievers will say, "This is a pitiless day!"

900 AD Tibet
Tibetans recorded stories of zombies called Ro-langs, literally "a risen corpse", that cannot speak, cannot bend at any joint, walk with stiff arms outstretched, only communicate by a wag of the tongue, and transmit their disease by touching a person's head. Still today, one can find low archways built to keep ro-langs from entering houses.

1200 AD Scandinavia
The Vikings recorded stories of zombies called Draugr, literally "one who walks after death". Draugrs are very strong, smell of decaying flesh, swell as though they are rotting, rise from the grave, spook animals, and feed on the flesh of their prey.

1503-1566 AD Nostradamus
The year the great seventh number is accomplished, appearing at the time of the great games of slaughter: not far from the age of the great millennium, when the dead will come out of their graves.

Modern Zombies

As recordkeeping and information dissemination technology evolves, the details of zombie encounters increase.

1980 Clairvius Narcisse

On May 2, 1962, at 1:15 PM, two attending physicians at Albert Schweitzer Hospital in Haiti pronounced Clairvius Narcisse dead. His sister identified his body and he was buried May 3rd, at 10:00 AM, in a family cemetery near l'Estere in the Artibonite Valley.

In 1980, 18 years later, he returned. Clairvius explained poisoning causing his paralysis. He heard the doctors declare him dead, felt the sheet go over his face, and felt the coffin nails as they were hammered into place. The night of his burial, he was taken from his grave to a plantation to work as a zombie slave, a fate from which he later escaped.

Family and a psychiatrist verified it was, in fact him.

1982 Obanis Pierre

Obanis Pierre died and was buried in Thomazeau, Haiti on October 13, 1977.

On February 19, 1982, Obanis was found to be alive at the Port-au-Price Center for Psychiatry and Neurology.

Obanis explained that he was called from his grave around eleven o'clock the night of his burial, then taken to a plantation to work. He was kept in a shed with four other zombies until the death of the land owner led to his freedom.

May 26, 2012 Miami, Florida

Rudy Eugene earned the nickname "Miami Zombie" by biting the face off Ronald Edward Poppo on the MacAruthur Causeway in Miami, Florida. At the end of the 18- minute attack, police intervened, ordering Rudy to stop. Rudy's response was to growl and go back to feeding on the face of his prey. The first shot by police did not deter the attacker. Four more shots were required to stop Rudy Eugene's attack.

May 31, 2012 Atlanta, Georgia

The United States Center for Disease Control and Prevention recognized the existence of zombies by reporting, "If you prepare for the zombie apocalypse, you will be prepared for all hazards."

April 5, 2012 Shrewsbury, Massachusetts

Jieming Liu was discovered in his home with blood on his hands and face, experiencing difficulty with communication and motor functions. His wife, Yuee Zhou, lay on the floor of another room of their home soaked in blood and missing her left arm below the elbow. In court, it was determined the missing flesh had been ingested by Jieming who died a month later.

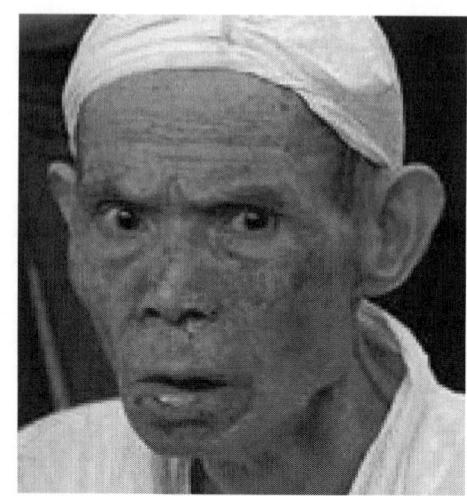

January 1, 2013
Zombies in Nature, The Washington Post
The Journal of Experimental Biology, January

"...the zombie apocalypse is old news in nature. There is a cadre of parasites, including viruses, fungi, protozoa, wasps and tapeworms, that hijack the nervous systems of their hosts, effectively zombifying them. Spiders in Costa Rica build webs for parasitic wasps living inside them. Horsehair worms compel hosts such as grasshoppers, which normally live on land, to enter water. A fungus takes over the abdomen of a cicada, leaving the head and thorax functional and the zombie cicada still able to fly. The parasites' purpose — to propagate their species — is no secret to scientists." – Maggie Fazeli Fard

February 14, 2013
Canada's House of Commons

"I do not need to tell you, Mr. Speaker, that zombies do not recognize borders and that a zombie invasion in the United States can easily turn into a continent-wide pandemic if it is not contained. So on behalf of concerned Canadians everywhere, I want to ask the Minister for Foreign Affairs, is he working with his American counterparts to develop an international zombie strategy so that a zombie invasion does not turn into a zombie apocalypse?"
– National Democratic Party Parliamentary Member Pat Martin

"Mr. Speaker, I want to assure this member, and all Canadians, that I am dead-icated to ensuring that this never happens. I want to say categorically to this member and through him to all Canadians that under the leadership of this Prime Minister, Canada will never become a safe haven for zombies, ever."
– Foreign Affairs Minister John Baird

POTENTIAL CAUSES OF THE ZOMBIE APOCALYPSE

The three major categories of theories predicting the cause of the zombie apocalypse are an act of God, a manmade pathogen, and a viral pandemic.

Act of God

Albert Einstein related, "My religion consists of a humble admiration of the illimitable superior spirit who reveals himself in the slight details we are able to perceive with our frail and feeble mind."

Those slight details reveal the creator, the illimitable superior spirit, God.

We live as amazing machines. The greatest of all animals, humans are the rightmost balance of all the details. The blood, heart, and circulation; the bones, joints, and muscles; the brain and nerves; the digestive system; the ears, nose, and throat; the endocrine system; the eyes and vision; the immune system; the kidneys and urinary system; the lungs and breathing; the reproductive system; the mouth and teeth; the skin, hair, and nails all combine cells, tissues, and membranes that function together to help us develop and stay healthy. The most complex organisms on our planet, we are constructed of trillions of microscopic parts, each with its own identity, working together in an organized manner for the benefit of the total being.

Faith aside, simply recognizing the complexity of the creation of the human body directs one to recognize that turning many of them into zombies would require another act of God.

Manmade Pathogen

Pathogens are bacteria, viruses, or microorganisms that can cause disease. Manmade pathogens can be biological or chemical.

An example of the ability for a manmade pathogen to create a zombie is based in the origin of the term zombie: Voodou. The Voodou religion is a combination of beliefs melding practices and rituals of varying schools of faith. One such practice is zombification. In Voodou, zombification is a method of dealing with out-of-hand people without killing them.

The tetrodotoxin neurotoxin poison of the puffer fish is administered to a human, simulating death. In a near death state, the human is subjected to hypnosis as a form of mind control. Voilá, a manmade zombie!

Haiti has so frequent problems with zombification that they made it a crime to turn someone into a zombie. Article 246 of the Haitian penal code states:

It shall also be qualified as attempted murder the employment which may be made against any person of substances which, without causing actual death, produce a lethargic coma more or less prolonged. If, after the person had been buried, the act shall be considered murder no matter what result follows.

And yet, still today, zombification is practiced by non-Haitians as hobbyists. One of the more famous was the serial killer, Jeffrey Dahmer. Overwhelmed with the task of disposing of dead bodies, Jeffrey Dahmer made several attempts to create a zombie sex slave by destroying the frontal lobe of several of his last victims. Using a drill, he created entryways into which he poured sulfuric acid into the skull. One such victim, Konerak Sinthasomphone, lived for some time after the somewhat successful zombification.

But, before we so harshly judge Jeffrey, let's not ignore the fact that the United States Central Intelligence Agency attempted to create zombies.

Starting in the early 1950's, the United States Central Intelligence Agency (CIA), through Project MKUltra, attempted to make zombies using manmade pathogens. One related memo, dated 1952, asked, *"Can we get control of an individual to the point where he will do our bidding against his will, and even against fundamental laws of nature, such as self-preservation?"*

As the CIA project progressed, the government tested drugs like LSD, temazepan, heroine, morphine, MDMA (ecstasy), mescaline, psilocybin, scopolamine, marijuana, alcohol, sodium pentothal, and ergine in an attempt, some say, to create a zombie army.

Today, street drugs going by the name bath salts and Anesthesia are based on these same manmade pathogens created by State sponsored bioengineers.

Viral Pandemic

Viral pandemics are viruses spreading over a wide geographic area affecting a large portion of the population. A viral pandemic is often nature driven, but stopped through manmade scientific solutions.

Around 1350, the Black Death, also known as the plague, killed about 100 million people, including over 30 percent of Europe's population. Including China, Central Asia, the Mediterranean, and Europe, this viral pandemic reduced the world population by about 25 percent.

In 1918, a viral flu pandemic, referred to as the Spanish Influenza, spread through World War I global military transportation. Within 2 years, about 15 percent of the world's population became infected, and about 5 percent of the world's population died. Death tolls included about 17 million in India, 390,000 in Japan, 1.5 million in Indonesia, over 500,000 in the United States, 50,000 in Canada, 250,000 in Britain, 400,000 in France, and untold numbers in Africa.

A recent spike in viruses capable of spreading over a wide geographic area, and affecting a large portion of the population, include such household threats as Ebola, HIV, Hendra, Swine Flu, Mad Cow Disease, and Rabies.

As with the Black Death and Spanish Influenza, these viruses are found to begin with animals and spread to humans. Mad Cow Disease, or bovine spongiform encephalopathy (BSE), kills cow brain cells, leaving sponge-like holes in the brain. A variant of BSE, Creutzfeldt-Jakob Disease (nvCJD), was found when several young people from the same areas as BSE outbreaks died of a brain disorder. The British government determined the cause of the human version of Mad Cow Disease was probably from the ingestion of meat from infected cows.

In 2003, the World Health Organization recognized Severe Acute Respiratory Syndrome (SARS), a virus that traveled the world very quickly from China to Hong Kong to Hanoi, to Vietnam in less than 2 weeks. Of the estimated 8,000 infections, there were 750 deaths.

The "H1Z1 virus" is the officially recognized term for the zombie virus.

Most Likely Cause of the Zombie Apocalypse

Because a manmade pathogen is not likely to spread globally, we're left with an act of God or a viral pandemic as the likely cause of the zombie apocalypse.

Steven C. Scilozman, MD, Harvard Medical School, states, "The most likely ideology for a zombie pandemic would be some kind of mutated contagion, most likely a virus".

Think Black Death and the Spanish Influenza, but with reanimation.

Dr. Robert Smith?, author of *Braaaiiinnnsss!: From Academics to Zobmies,* from The Department of Mathematics at The University of Ottawa, states, "a disease that works through just direct human contact can actually spread remarkably efficiently". He adds, "it is (gestation period) almost certainly going to be very, very rapid; maximum 24 hours."

As such, a city of half a million inhabitants will be either dead or zombified within about 7 days. A city the size of New York would only require between 8 or 9 days.

WATCH FOR SIGNS

To the untrained, social media will be the first indicator of the zombie apocalypse outbreak. By the time you are reading about it on Facebook, it is too late.

Due to economic, political, social, and religious concerns, the world's governments will not warn you in enough time to safely avoid outbreaks. All of the world's governments know it is coming, and so do we, but the question is, WHEN? Your goal is to identify the outbreak before it becomes local to you. To do so, you will need to apply the following tips to read between the lines of what the government, via the news media, is presenting.

TIP 1: Government Denial. The 1918 Spanish Influenza got its name because Spain was one of the few countries in the world without an active press sponsorship. How long did the world's governments hide information about the Spanish Influenza; information that could have saved hundreds of thousands of lives? Every time the government vehemently denies a concern for a zombie apocalypse, remind yourself that denial is the first tactic to control the citizens.

TIP 2: Inexplicable Diseases. With modern technology, inexplicable diseases are few and far between. Comparing domestic news coverage to the news coverage local to the disease outbreak can allow you to identify potential inconsistencies suggesting a zombie outbreak.

TIP 3: Military Deployments. The world's governments have always deployed military forces to clean up zombie hotspots as the first defense against a global outbreak. Zombies are our one true global foe. Anywhere that two or more countries are working together on a military objective, you can fairly conclude a zombie outbreak is involved. If they are not responding to an outbreak, they are probably using the undead as subversive weapons.

TIP 4: Mass Killings. Someone find a group of slaughtered people? No one taking the credit? You can bet that soon enough you will read that it is associated with a drug cartel or a couple bad apples gone rotten. Do not believe it. It is not unusual for people just like you and me to identify and eliminate an outbreak before it gets out of hand. Labeled crazies and murderers, the world has a long history of locking up its first line of zombie defense.

TIP 5: Concentrated Inhuman Crimes. Face-eating drug addicts, religious mass suicides, and other crimes of horrendous brutality can be possible acts of one or more zombies. Watch for crimes like these in concentrated areas.

Be aware, the signs are there.

STAY AHEAD OF THE OUTBREAK

Unless you are living in a large city or near a major transit hub, combining incidents of suspicious activities with geographic mapping should result in your accurately predicting the oncoming nightmare of the undead days before it spreads to your state, and enough hours before it affects your neighborhood.

If you fail at your own efforts to identify and track outbreaks, and if you fail to adequately read the signs, and you are not already a zombie or zombie food, you are probably going to be one of the unlucky who finally get the Truth through the eventual United Nations Declaration of a Global War on Zombies.

ZOMBIE PREPAREDNESS

Zombies have existed since the earliest of recorded history, they exist today, and the Earth's population growth combined with global travel and trade is getting closer to exposing everyone on our planet to their disease more so than ever before. It is not entirely a fictional basis that prompts writers, film makers, and the general public to daily produce more zombie survival training and educational material. Zombie Preparedness is not a passing fad; it is a prediction of the coming apocalypse.

By understanding the psychology of survival, planning to survive, putting that plan into action, applying survival medical procedures, finding water and food, defending yourself, successfully moving in zombie infested areas, and establishing a long term zombie apocalypse retreat, you can still survive.

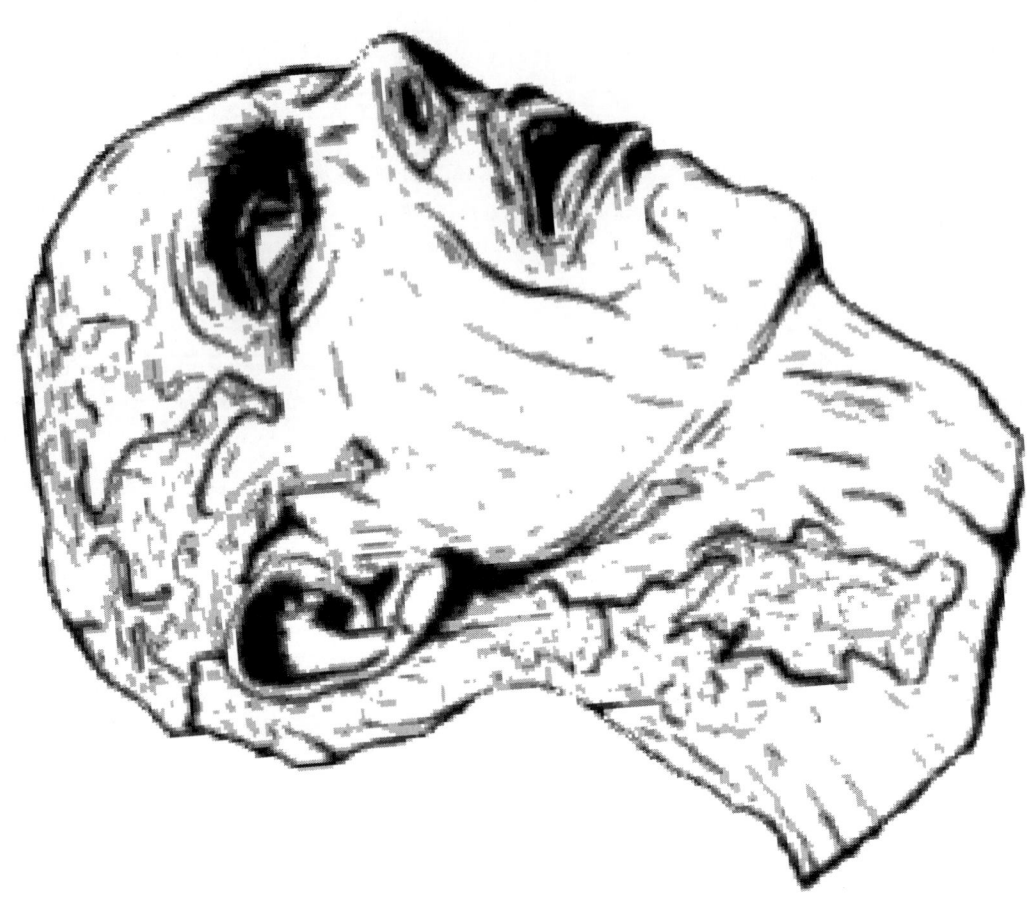

For the untrained, social media will be the first indicator of the zombie apocalypse. When panic erupts, most will try to flee, but panic will be so widespread, trying to escape will lead to failure. Society will hurt itself as it attempts to avoid the stumbling, ravenously hungry corpses.

In areas of low population, everyone staying put and avoiding each other could limit the spread of infection enough that local government officials could contain the outbreak. But, what is the likelihood of everyone having the psychological fortitude to stay put?

2 – PSYCHOLOGY OF ZOMBIE SURVIVAL

Surviving a zombie apocalypse requires more than the knowledge and skills to find defensible shelter, food, and water, while traveling through areas occupied by the undead. How have uneducated people, with little or no zombie survival training, managed to survive undead outbreaks while others, with zombie survival training, have not used their skills and died at the hands and bites of the flesh eaters? A key ingredient in any zombie survival situation is the mental attitude of the individual involved. Having zombie survival skills is important; having the will to survive the zombie apocalypse is essential. Without a desire to survive the undead, acquired skills serve little purpose and invaluable knowledge goes to waste. **Zombie Survival Will is Essential**.

There is a psychology to zombie survival. You will face many stressors in a walking rotting corpse infected environment that ultimately will affect your mind. Stressors can produce thoughts and emotions that, if poorly understood, can transform a confident, well-trained person into an indecisive, ineffective liability with questionable ability to avoid and survive the gnashing teeth and outreached hands of the zombie masses. Thus, you must be aware of, and be able to recognize, those stressors commonly associated with zombie survival.

It is also imperative that you be aware of your reactions to the wide variety of stressors associated with zombie outbreaks. This chapter identifies and explains the nature of stress, the stressors of zombie survival, and those internal reactions that you will naturally experience when faced with the stressors of a real-world outbreak.

Recognize and prepare for stress, as, like the soulless human corpses, it will come from every direction. In our pre-zombie-apocalyptic minds, long work hours, traffic jams, marital discord, finances, and the occasional bout with the flu are common stressors. During the zombie apocalypse, nearly everyone on the globe will experience fatigue due to the lack of nutrition; watch neighbors, friends, and family being attacked by zombies and reanimating as the enemy; see seemingly minor injuries like a bite result in euthanasia; lose their homes to the invading hordes of death reanimated; and experience isolation for so many days that they'll wonder if the only survivors on Earth are the ones holed up with them in their damp storm shelter.

A LOOK AT STRESS

Before we can understand our psychological reactions in a zombie infested environment, it is helpful to first know a little bit about stress and its effects. Like zombism, stress is not a disease that you cure and eliminate. Instead, it is a condition all living experience. Stress is our reaction to pressure. It is the name given to the experience we have as we physically, mentally, emotionally, and spiritually respond to life's tensions, like undead aggressors.

NEED FOR STRESS

We need stress because it has many positive benefits. Stress provides us with challenges; it gives us chances to learn about our values and strengths. Stress can show our ability to handle pressure without breaking; without succumbing to the undead. It tests our adaptability and flexibility, and can stimulate us to do our best. Because we usually do not consider unimportant events stressful, stress can also be an excellent indicator of the significance we attach to an event—in other words, it highlights what is important to us.

We need to have some stress in our lives, but, like zombies, too much of anything can be detrimental. The goal is to have stress, but not an excess of it. Too much stress can take its toll on people and groups. Too much stress leads to distress. Distress causes an uncomfortable tension that, like the undead, we try to escape, or preferably, avoid.

Listed below are a few of the common signs of distress associated with too much zombie stress:

- Difficulty making decisions regarding the living and the undead
- Angry outbursts
- Forgetfulness
- Low energy level
- Constant worrying about zombies
- Propensity for mistakes
- Thoughts about death or suicide
- Trouble and withdrawing from the living
- Hiding from responsibilities
- Carelessness with both the living and undead

Stress can be constructive or destructive. It can encourage or discourage, move us along to stop the undead in their tracks, or stop us dead in our tracks, and make life meaningful or seemingly meaningless. Stress can inspire you to operate successfully and perform at your maximum zombie-surviving efficiency. It can also cause you to panic and forget all your zombie survival training. Your key to survival is your ability to manage the inevitable stresses. The person that survives a zombie outbreak is one who works with stress instead of letting stress work on them.

SURVIVAL STRESSORS

Any zombie related event can lead to stress, and, as many a survivor has experienced, zombies do not always come one at a time. Often, stressful events occur simultaneously. These events are not stress, but they produce it and are called "stressors." Stressors are the obvious cause while stress is the response. Once the body recognizes the presence of a stressor, like an approaching walking corpse, it begins to act to protect itself.

In response to a zombie stressor, the body prepares to "fight or flee." This preparation involves an internal signal for help sent throughout the body. The response is the following actions:

- The body releases stored fuels (sugar and fats) to provide quick energy.
- Breathing rate increases to supply more oxygen to the blood.
- Muscle tension increases to prepare for action.
- Blood clotting mechanisms are activated to reduce bleeding from cuts.
- Senses become more acute (hearing becomes more sensitive, pupils dilate, smell becomes sharper) so that you are more aware of your zombie infested surroundings.
- Heart rate and blood pressure rise to provide more blood to the muscles.

This protective posture lets you cope with potential zombie dangers. However, you cannot maintain this level of alertness indefinitely.

Stressors are not courteous; one zombie does not leave because another arrives. Zombies add up. The cumulative effect of minor stressors can be a major distress if they happen too close together. As the body's resistance to the stress of a zombie outbreak wears down, and the sources of stress (zombies) continue (or increase), eventually a state of exhaustion arrives. At this point, the ability to resist stress or use it in a positive way gives out and signs of distress appear. Anticipating zombie stressors and developing strategies to cope with them are two ingredients in the effective management of stress. Therefore, it is essential that you be aware of the types of stressors that you will encounter. The following paragraphs explain a few of these.

Injury, Illness, Zombie Infection, Death, and the Undead

Injury, illness, zombie infection, death, and the undead are real threats that you will face. Perhaps nothing is more stressful than being alone in an unfamiliar environment where you could die from zombie aggression, an accident, or from ingesting something lethal. Illness and injury can also add to stress by limiting your ability to maneuver, get food and drink, find shelter, and defend yourself. Even if illness and injury do not lead to death, they add to stress through the pain and discomfort they generate. It is only by controlling the stress associated with your vulnerability to injury, illness, zombie infection, death, and the undead that you can have the courage to take the risks associated with surviving the undead.

Uncertainty and Lack of Control

Some living have trouble operating in settings where everything is not clear-cut. The only guarantee in a zombie situation is that nothing is guaranteed. It can be extremely stressful operating on limited information in a setting where you have limited control of your surroundings. This uncertainty and lack of control also add to the stress of being ill, injured, infected, or killed.

Environment

Even under the most ideal circumstances, nature is quite formidable. To survive the zombie apocalypse, you will have to contend with the stressors of weather, terrain, and the variety of zombies inhabiting an area. Heat, cold, rain, winds, mountains, swamps, deserts, insects, dangerous reptiles, zombies, renegade militia, animals, and other dangers are just a few of the challenges that you will encounter while working to survive the zombie apocalypse. Depending on how you handle the stress of your environment, your surroundings can be either a source of food and protection, or the cause of extreme discomfort leading to injury, illness, infection, or death.

Hunger and Thirst

Unlike the undead, without food and water you will weaken and eventually die. Thus, getting and preserving food and water takes on increasing importance as the length of time in a zombie survival setting increases. Foraging can also be a big source of stress since you are used to buying your food in stores, not hunting and scrounging while defending yourself from the soulless shuffling corpses.

Fatigue

Forcing yourself to continue surviving the zombie apocalypse is not easy as you grow more tired. It is possible to become so fatigued that the act of just staying awake is stressful in itself.

Isolation

There are some advantages to facing adversity with others. As a survivor you learn individual skills, but you should train to function as part of a team. Being in contact with other survivalists provides a greater sense of security and a feeling someone is available to help if problems occur. A significant stressor in zombie survival situations is that often you have to rely solely on your own resources. Sometimes, you *are* the help.

The zombie survival stressors mentioned in this chapter are by no means the only ones you may face. Remember, what is stressful to one person may not be stressful to another. Different people will react differently to the new stressors. Be prepared for your closest friends to see you differently once you bludgeon an infected child's brain. We will all be experiencing a new level of stressors, so keep an open mind to how others will handle the fear, fatigue, hunger, shuffling dead, depression, anger, boredom, sleep deprivation, and isolation. Your experiences, training, personal outlook on life, physical and mental conditioning, and level of self-confidence contribute to what you will find stressful in a zombie infested environment. The object is not to avoid stress, but rather to manage the stressors of zombies and make them work for you.

We now have a general knowledge of stress and the stressors common to survival. The next step is to examine your reactions to the stressors you may face.

KEEP A COOL HEAD

Regardless of how many movies you have watched, how many pig heads you have speared, and the thousands of rounds you shot at the range, nothing can compare you to the undead combat you will encounter. Seeing or living through an event that caused or threatened serious harm or death is never easy. To help prepare yourself for combat with the undead, remember these tips:

- **Keep your head where your feet are**. Focusing on the image of six flesh eaters gnawing at your neighbor's corpse, or worrying about who or what you will find at your next shelter will only distract you from the immediate task at hand. With one foot in the past, and the other in the future, all you are doing is pissing on the present.

- **They are already dead**. Too many seasoned zombie survivalists have fallen to mislead momentary belief that they saw a glimpse of humanity in their approaching predator. Zombies are clinically proven to have no memory of their human lives. They cannot be tamed. They cannot be trained. Do not hesitate to put a zombie out of its misery.

- **Never give up**. Zombies exist for one task, eating flesh. Psychological warfare does not apply; they do not care about threats or promises. Fear does not apply to them; they do not care about physical harm. A supply chain means nothing to them; they do not care about food or water or gas or shelter. Nothing distracts them from their goal of eating you. Imagine a rotten fleshy version of the Terminator, or Yule Brenner in Westworld. As such, you cannot surrender. Never give up.

NATURAL REACTIONS

Humankind has been able to survive many zombie outbreaks throughout the centuries. Our ability to adapt physically and mentally to a zombie infested world kept us alive while other species around us perished. The same survival mechanisms that kept our forefathers alive can help keep you alive as well! However, the zombie survival mechanisms that can help you can also work against you if you do not understand and anticipate their presence.

It is not surprising that the average person will have some psychological reactions to a zombie situation. The following paragraphs explain some of the major internal reactions that you, or anyone with you, might experience with the previously stated zombie stressors.

Fear

Fear is our emotional response to dangerous zombie circumstances that we believe have the potential to cause death, injury, infection, or illness. This harm is not just limited to physical damage; the threat to your emotional and mental well-being can generate fear as well. If you are trying to survive a zombie outbreak, fear can have a positive function if it encourages you to be cautious in situations where recklessness could result in injury, infection and death. Unfortunately, fear can also immobilize you. It can cause you to become so frightened that you fail to perform activities essential for survival. Most people will have some degree of fear when placed in unfamiliar surroundings under zombie conditions. There is no shame in this! You must train yourself not to be overcome by your fears of the undead. Desensitize yourself by watching as many zombie movies as you can get your hands on, but remember to critically sort through the fictional trash, keeping only the treasure of learning from the characters' experiences. Ideally, through watching many movies and conducting hands-on, realistic training, you can acquire the knowledge and skills needed to increase your confidence and thereby manage your zombie fears.

Anxiety

Associated with fear is anxiety. Because it is natural for you to be afraid of zombies, it is also natural for you to experience anxiety. Anxiety can be an uneasy, apprehensive feeling you get when faced with dangerous zombie situations (physical, mental, and emotional). When used in a healthy way, anxiety can urge you to act to end, or at least master, the dangers that threaten your existence. If you were never anxious, there would be little motivation to make changes in your life. In a zombie survival setting you can reduce your anxiety by performing those tasks that will ensure you come through the ordeal alive. As you reduce your anxiety, you also bring under control the source of that anxiety—your fears of the undead. In this form, anxiety is good; however, anxiety can also have a devastating impact. Anxiety can overwhelm you to the point where you become easily confused and have difficulty thinking. Once this happens, it will become increasingly difficult for you to make good judgments and sound decisions about zombies. To survive, you must learn techniques to calm your anxieties and keep them in the range where they help, not hurt.

Anger and Frustration

Frustration arises when you are continually thwarted by the aggressive undead in your attempts to reach a goal. The goal of survival is to stay alive until you can retreat. To achieve this goal, you must complete some tasks with minimal resources. It is inevitable, in trying to do these tasks, that something will go wrong; that something will happen beyond your control; and as such, with your life at stake, every mistake is magnified in terms of its importance. Thus, eventually, you will have to cope with frustration when a few of your plans run into the undead. One outgrowth of this frustration is anger. There are many events in a zombie situation that can frustrate or anger you. Getting lost, damaged or forgotten equipment, the weather, inhospitable terrain, renegade militia, zombified relatives and friends, and physical limitations are just a few sources of frustration and anger. Frustration and anger generate impulsive reactions, irrational behavior, poorly thought-out decisions, and, in some instances, an "I quit, just eat me" attitude. People sometimes avoid doing something they cannot master. If you can harness and properly channel the emotional intensity associated with anger and frustration, you can productively act as you answer the challenges of surviving the zombie apocalypse. If you do not properly focus your angry feelings, you can waste much energy and resources in activities that do little to further either your chances of surviving the zombies or the chances of those around you.

Depression

You would be a rare person indeed if you did not get sad, at least momentarily, when faced with the hardships of a zombie outbreak. As this sadness deepens, it becomes "depression." Depression is closely linked with frustration and anger. Frustration will cause you to become increasingly angry as you fail to reach your survival goals. If the anger does not help you succeed, then the frustration level goes even higher. A destructive cycle between anger and frustration will continue until you become worn down—physically, emotionally, and mentally. When you reach this point, you start to give up, and your focus shifts from "What can I do about these zombies" to "There is nothing I can do about these damned zombies." Depression is an expression of this hopeless, helpless feeling. There is nothing wrong with being sad as you temporarily think about your loved ones and remember what life was like back in "civilization" or "the pre-apocalyptic world." Such thoughts, in fact, can give you the desire to try harder and live one more day, through one more encounter with the reanimated. On the other hand, if you allow yourself to sink into a depressed state, it can drain your energy and, more important, your will to survive. It is imperative that you resist succumbing to depression.

Loneliness and Boredom

The living are social animals. The living enjoy the company of others. Very few people want to be alone all the time. There is a distinct chance of isolation in a zombie survival setting. Isolation is not bad. Loneliness and boredom can bring to the surface qualities you thought only others had. The extent of your imagination and creativity may surprise you. When required to do so, you may discover some hidden talents and abilities. Most of all, you may tap into a reservoir of inner strength and fortitude you never knew you had. Conversely, loneliness and boredom can be another source of depression. If you are surviving alone, or with others, you must find ways to keep your mind productively occupied. Additionally, you must develop a degree of self-sufficiency. You must have faith in your capability to face the stumbling, ravenously hungry corpses alone.

Guilt

The circumstances leading to your being in a zombie infested setting are sometimes dramatic and tragic. It may be the result of a viral pandemic and one wrong turn, or an accident. Perhaps you were the only survivor, or one of a few survivors. While naturally relieved to be alive, you simultaneously may be mourning the deaths and reanimation of others who were less fortunate. It is not uncommon for survivors to feel guilty about being spared from zombism while others were not. This feeling, when used in a positive way, has encouraged people to try harder to survive with the belief they were allowed to live for some greater purpose in life. Sometimes, survivors of zombie outbreaks tried to stay alive so that they could carry on the work of those added to the undead masses. Whatever reason you give yourself, do not let guilt prevent you from living. The living who abandon their chance to survive the zombie apocalypse accomplish nothing. Such an act would be the greatest tragedy.

PREPARING YOURSELF

Your mission in a zombie survival situation is to stay alive without infection. The assortment of thoughts and emotions you will experience in a zombie situation can work for you, or they can work to your downfall. Fear, anxiety, anger, frustration, guilt, depression, and loneliness are all possible reactions to the many stressors common to zombie survival. These reactions, when controlled in a healthy way, help to increase your likelihood of surviving. They prompt you to pay more attention in training, to fight back when scared, to take actions that ensure sustenance and security, to keep faith with your fellow team members, and to strive against large odds, like a horde of the flesh eating, soulless, reanimated corpses. When you cannot control these reactions in a healthy way, they can bring you to a standstill. Instead of rallying your internal resources, you listen to your internal fears. These fears will cause you to experience psychological defeat long before you physically succumb. Remember, survival is natural to everyone; being unexpectedly thrust into the life-or-death struggle of surviving the zombie apocalypse is not. Do not be afraid of your natural reactions to this unnatural situation. Prepare yourself to rule over these reactions so they serve your ultimate interest—staying alive and uninfected.

Being prepared involves knowing that your reactions in a zombie setting are productive, not destructive. The challenges of the undead have produced countless examples of heroism, courage, and self-sacrifice. These are the qualities a zombie situation can bring out in you if you have prepared yourself. Below are a few tips to help psychologically prepare for zombies. By studying this book and attending survival training you can develop the "zombie survival attitude."

Know Yourself

Be realistic. Not all of us are soldiers, or hunters, or mechanics, or sharpshooters, or medics. You should take the time, through training, and discussions with family, and friends to discover who you are on the inside. Know your skills and limits. Strengthen your stronger qualities and develop the areas that you know are necessary to survive the undead. Appendix B – Goal Setting includes an exercise to guide your efforts to become a balanced whole-survivalist.

Anticipate Fears

Do not pretend that you will have no fears of the dead reanimated. Begin thinking about what would frighten you the most about zombies, if forced to survive alone. Train in those areas of concern to you. The goal is not to eliminate the fear of zombies, but to build confidence in your ability to function despite your fears of the undead.

Adopt A Positive Attitude

Learn to see the potential good in everything. Looking for the good not only boosts morale, it is excellent for exercising your imagination and creativity. Singing songs, only when certain you are not in any danger of attracting the flesh eaters, can lift spirits.

Suggested songs include:

- Joy to the World (Three Dog Night)
- Put One Foot In Front Of The Other (Mickey Rooney and Keenan Wynn)
- Where's Your Head At (Basement Jaxx)
- Somewhere Over The Rainbow (Judy Garland or Israel Kamakawiwo'ole)
- What Doesn't Kill You (Stronger) (Kelly Clarkson)
- Do not Stop Me Now (Queen)
- Three Little Birds (Bob Marley)
- Do not Worry, Be Happy (Bobby McFerrin)
- Beautiful Day (U2)
- I Can See Clearly Now (Johnny Nash)
- Walking On Sunshine (Katrina And The Waves)
- You Are My Sunshine (Jimmie Davis)
- What A Wonderful World (Louis Armstrong)

Be Realistic

Do not be afraid to make an honest appraisal of zombie situations. See circumstances as they are, not as you want them to be. Keep your hopes and expectations within the estimate of the situation. When you go into a zombie setting with unrealistic expectations, you may be laying the groundwork for bitter disappointment, infection, or death. Follow the adage, "Hope for the best, prepare for the undead." It is much easier to adjust to pleasant surprises about your unexpected good fortunes than to be upset by your unexpected harsh circumstances.

Remind Yourself What Is At Stake

Failure to prepare psychologically to cope with stumbling, rotting, flesh eating corpses leads to reactions such as depression, carelessness, inattention, loss of confidence, poor decision making, and giving up before the body gives in. Remember that your life and the lives of others who depend on you are at stake.

Train

Through zombie survival training and life experiences, begin today to prepare to cope with the rigors of the undead. Demonstrating your skills in training will give you the confidence to call upon them should the need arise. Remember, the more realistic the training, the less overwhelming an actual zombie outbreak will be.

Learn Stress Management Techniques

People under stress have a potential to panic if they are not well-trained and not prepared psychologically to face the staggering, rotting corpses. While you often cannot control the undead with which you find yourself, it is within your ability to control your response to the reanimated. Learning stress management techniques can significantly enhance your capability to remain calm and focused as you work to keep yourself and others alive. A few good techniques to develop include zombie combat skills, relaxation skills, time management skills, assertiveness skills, and cognitive restructuring skills (the ability to control how you view a situation). Remember, "the will to survive" can also be considered "the refusal to give in to the undead."

In the debilitating chaos of the zombie apocalypse, civilian governments and authorities will fail to function effectively. Marshall Law, military rule by military authorities, will be imposed. There will be immediate government responses, but eventually the spread will outgrow the government's ability to contain the outbreak.

Banks will be overrun. Transportation systems will gridlock. Power grids will shut down. Water and septic pumps will stop. Internet and telephone communications will falter. Perishable food will spoil. Civilization will turn on itself.

Prepared survivalists will rise above the chaos to preserve what is left of society.

3 - SURVIVAL PLANNING

A zombie survival plan is dependent on three separate but intertwined parts to be successful: planning, preparation, and practice. Surviving the zombie apocalypse is the culmination of all we do to prepare and survive.

Proper planning prevents poor performance. Zombie survival planning is nothing more than realizing you will one day find yourself in the middle of a zombie outbreak, and, with that in mind, taking steps to increase your chances of survival. It can happen to anyone, anywhere, anytime, so remember: **failure to plan is a plan to fail**. Zombie survival plans are based on undead evasion considerations and the availability of resupply or emergency resources. You must take into consideration the bug out and travelling duration, and the distance to safe areas; the environment, to include the terrain and weather and possible changes in the weather during a protracted survival period; and the form of transportation you will be operating with, such as a motorized vehicle, bicycle, or perhaps just hiking boots. Planning also entails looking at routes and knowing by memory the major geographical features in case your gps, map and compass are lost. You can use sources such as the Internet, guidebooks, and maps to assist you in zombie apocalypse planning.

Preparation means preparing yourself and your zombie survival kit for contingencies in your plan. A zombie apocalypse survival plan without preparation is just a piece of paper. It will not keep you among the dwindling ranks of the living. Prepare yourself by making sure your immunizations and dental work are up-to-date. Break in your hiking boots and make sure they have good soles and water-repellent properties. Study the area, climate, terrain, and indigenous sources of food and water. Continuously assess data, even after the zombie apocalypse survival plan is made, to update the plan as necessary to give you the greatest possible chance of survival. Practice those things that you have planned with the items in your zombie survival kit. Testing ensures that items work and that you know how to use them. Hike five miles and build a fire in the rain so you know when it is critical to get warm, you can do it. Review the medical items in your kit and have instructions printed on their use so that even in times of stress, you will not make life-threatening errors.

IMPORTANCE OF PLANNING

Detailed planning is essential in zombie survival situations. Including undead considerations in survival planning will enhance your chances of living when the outbreak occurs. For example, if your bug out location requires that you stay in a small, enclosed area that limits what you can carry on your person, plan where you can put your backpack. Put it where it will not prevent you from getting out of the area quickly to avoid the flesh eaters, yet where it is readily accessible when the reanimated eventually find you.

One important aspect of zombie survival planning is preventive medicine. Ensuring that you have no dental problems and that your immunizations are current will help you avoid potential dental or health problems outside of the zombie attacks. Some dental problems can progress to the point that you may not be able to eat enough to survive. Failure to keep your shots current may mean your body is not immune to the other, non-zombic, diseases prevalent in the area.

Provide future instructions if you want fellow zombie survivalists to apply brain destroying measures in certain situations. Talk to your fellow zombie survivalists about what these terms mean. The Advance Undead Directive (Appendix A) states what choices you would have made for yourself if you were reanimated. Talk to your family members, friends, and others you trust about your choices. Also, it is a good idea to talk with professionals such as your doctors, clergypersons, and lawyers before you complete this Undead Will.

Preparing and carrying a zombie survival kit is as important as preventive medical considerations. Most government buildings have basic zombie survival kits for the local area. There are kits for hot climate and cold climate zombie survival. Know the location of these kits and what they contain in case of an outbreak of soulless human corpses. There are also military kits for tropical and moderate climate survival. These kits are expensive and not always available to every survivor. However, if you know what these kits contain, and on what basis they are built, you will be able to plan and to prepare your own zombie survival kit that may be better suited to you than an off-the-shelf solution.

Even the smallest zombie survival kit, if properly prepared, is invaluable when faced with the problem of the shuffling rotting corpses. However, before making your zombie survival kit, consider your overall zombie apocalypse survival plan.

Survival Kits

The environment is the key to the types of items you will need in your zombie survival kit. How much equipment you put in your zombie kit depends on how you will carry the kit. A kit carried on your body will have to be smaller than one carried in a vehicle. Always layer your survival kit—body, load-bearing vest or equipment, and mode of transportation (motorized vehicle, bicycle, or hiking). Keep the most important items on your body. For example, your map and compass should always be on your body, as should your basic life-sustaining items (knife, lighter). Carry less important items on your vehicle. Place bulky items in the backpack.

In preparing your zombie survival kit, select items that are multipurpose, compact, lightweight, durable, and most importantly, functional. An item is not good if it looks great but doesn't perform as designed. Items should complement each other from layer to layer. A lighter in your pocket can be augmented by a magnesium bar with your vehicle and additional dry tinder in your backpack.

Your zombie survival kit need not be elaborate. You need only functional items that will meet your needs and a case to hold the items. For the case, you might want to use a bandage box, soap dish, tobacco tin, first-aid case, ammunition pouch, or another suitable case. This case should be—

- Blood-repellent and waterproof
- Easy to carry or attach to your body
- Suitable to accept various-sized components
- Durable enough to sustain the reanimated's death grip

Your zombie survival kit should be broken down into the following categories:

- Water
- Fire
- Zombie Defensive Shelter
- Food
- Medical
- Miscellaneous

Each category should contain items that allow you to sustain your basic needs. For example, water—you should have items that allow you to scoop up, draw up, soak up, or suck up water; something to gather rainwater, condensation, or perspiration; something to transport water; and something to purify or filter water.

Examples of each category in a zombie survival kit are as follows:

- Water—purification tablets, bleach, povidone-iodine drops, sponges, small plastic or rubber tubing, collapsible canteens or water bags.

- Fire—lighter, metal match, waterproof matches, magnesium bar, candle, magnifying lens.

- Zombie Defensive Shelter— parachute cord, large knife, machete or hatchet, poncho, space blanket, hammock, mosquito net, tarp, wire saw.

- Food—knife, snare wire, fishhooks, fish and snare line, bouillon cubes or soup packets, high-energy food bars, granola bars, aluminum foil, freezer bags.

- Medical—oxytetracycline tablets (to treat diarrhea or infection), surgical blades or surgical preparation knife, butterfly sutures, lip balm, safety pins, sutures, antidiarrheal medication (imodium), broad-spectrum antibiotics (rocephin and zithromax) and broad spectrum topical ophthalmic (eye) antibiotic (not that they'll be useful against a zombie-initiated infection), antifungal, anti-inflammatory (ibuprofen), petrolatum gauze, and soap. Medical items may make up approximately 50 percent of your survival kit.

- Miscellaneous—wrist compass, needle and thread, eyeglasses, knife sharpener, cork, binoculars, sleeping bag, toolkit, and this Zombie Preparedness Guide.

Of course, include a wise selection of aggressive rotting corpse defensive weapons, as the situation so dictates. Weapons will be covered more in depth in the Zombie Combat chapter. Read and practice the zombie survival techniques in this book and apply these basic concepts to those you read about in other zombie apocalypse survival resources. Consider your survival and the environment in which you will defend yourself against the ever-advancing hordes of the flesh eating reanimated. Imagination may be the largest part of your kit. It can replace many of the items in a kit. Combined with the will to live, it can mean the difference between surviving to one day live without the horror of the walking soulless human corpses or joining your undead neighbors in their flesh eating aggression towards the living until a better prepared survivor puts you out of your infected misery.

Consider maintaining multiple zombie survival kits, as the outbreak can happen at any time. Keeping kits at your work, in your car, and at home will ensure you are rarely unprepared.

TEAMWORK

You cannot do this alone. The group dynamics of surviving the zombie apocalypse are not unlike those of working through an obstacle course. The successful survivors will incorporate a mixture of effective leadership, buddy systems, trust, teamwork, and encouragement.

DOn't wa**IT**. Recruit your team right now. Some zombie apocalypse survival team member skills you should include are:

Medical Professional. Someone skilled and experienced with tourniquets, stitches, sprains, antibiotics, broken bones, sprained ankles, and traumatic injuries can support a team's medical needs.

Leader. A natural example of the ethics and morals you will want from your team, combined with the proven ability to teach others to rise to greater heights, the willingness to accept responsibility for the group, a supportive attitude, and a commitment to the better good of the team are the characteristics you will want in your leadership.

Outdoor Survivalist. This is the person who knows how to build a fire in the rain, how to build a lean-to out of a pile of sticks and some leaves, which plants are poisonous, how to cook a worm, and how to build a raft out of fallen trees. When the zhit hits the fan, you are going to want an outdoor survivalist on your team.

Hunter. The right mixture of skill, technique, patience, and experience make a great hunter. Land and weather environments, an understanding of the local wildlife, the skills of calling and shooting, being patient and quiet, running prey with dogs, and even as basic as choosing the appropriate weapon are all factors a good hunter understands. Instinct is another invaluable characteristic of a successful hunter. How do some hunters know which direction the animals will be turning half a mile in advance? Hunting can be the difference between a group's life and death. You will want a successful hunter on your team.

Warrior. Honor, courage, and commitment alone do not make a great zombie warrior. You will want a warrior with a demonstrated ruthlessness in dealing with the undead, a mastery of the appropriate effective zombie weaponry, fighting discipline to the point of savagery when necessary, a willingness to die for the security of the group, a stealthy movement ability, and the ability to command and train others to help. Battle-hardened zombie warriors with proven tactics will be hard to find at first, but every zombie warrior must start somewhere, so make sure your team's warrior has real-life military battle experience, spends what seems like an unhealthy amount of time at the gun range, and includes crushing pig skulls as a hobby. Your team will benefit by having a great warrior.

Mechanic. Most machines are made of nuts, bolts, gears, oil, rubber, plastic, water, and gas. While this may seem a simple enough list of parts, knowing how they all work together as a motorized vehicle, water pump, electric generator, or chainsaw is the skillset of a mechanic. A great mechanic should have a natural aptitude to identify, repair and replace failing components; and perform scheduled maintenance. Maintaining engines, suspensions, transmissions, steering components, electrical systems, breaking systems, and cooling systems should all be second nature. Diagnostic skills, measuring tools and methods, an understanding of how stuff works, and the ability to execute a repair are all signs of a great mechanic. That friend of yours who is not scared to roll up their sleeves and tackle a transmission replacement is a great starting point for filling the mechanic position on your team. While machines are not the ultimate solution to avoiding or combatting zombies, mechanical know-how will make some survival tasks easier.

Notes about choosing your team members:

- Some members of your team will play dual roles. Hunters often make great warriors.
- No one should specialize; everyone should cross train. Having one mechanic puts you one soulless human corpse bite away from losing your mechanic.
- Everyone should be physically capable of sprinting, hiking long distances, carrying their own backpacks, lifting themselves over fences, and bicycling long distances.
- Skinny people will not last as long. Without some fat on their bodies, once their food is scarce, people with low body fat will start to feel the effects of starving first. A whole-person healthiness is the rightmost goal for the pre-outbreak world.
- Once your team is assembled, and as you add and remove members, retrain everyone as a group. The team that trains together survives the zombie apocalypse together.
- Practice with your weapons together, in lifelike situations, no less than monthly.

- An annual DISC assessment will help the team effectively handle different behaviors of the individual team members in a group environment. Wouldn't it suck try to deal with incompatible member behaviors while also dealing with a flesh eater scratching at your door?

BUG OUT LOCATION

Zombie apocalypse bug out locations will be your protective home for no less than the first seven days of the outbreak's reaching your local area. As such, choosing and preparing this location is a key step towards adequately preparing for your survival.

Follow this guidance when picking the bug out location best suited for you.

- Decide now who is joining you. Are you going solo, will it only be your team members, or will your team members be bringing family? An absolute head count will be necessary to pick the best location.
- Choose a location large enough to house everyone in your expected group.
- Taking all other factors into account, get as far away from a major city and major roads as reasonable.
- Distance from your daily routine is a factor. You will want to be able to get there within 12 hours. Take the route into account; bridges, tunnels, weather, and natural formations can create bottlenecks of death.
- Property immediately next to federal and state parks helps expand the usable footprint beyond its property lines.
- Fresh water is a near necessity. Best case scenario, establish a well with both a mechanical and manual pump. Worst case scenario should be limited to walking one mile for water.
- Concealed sites help minimize visits; not just from the stumbling, ravenously hungry corpses, but humans liabilities, too.
- With so many abandoned buildings, shelter from the elements should be easy, but a successful survivor should still plan for the cold and heat.
- In case of evacuation, a bug out location with one way in and two ways out can save lives

- Sleeping in a boat anchored in the middle of a lake may seem like a great solution, but the human body floats 3 days after a drowning. Even without swimming, a zombie can randomly float its way to your boat, resulting in a rude awakening.
- Camp the prospective area now to get a sense of the property and local people.
- Own the property now, if you can afford it. Document the legal arrangement now. Once the outbreak starts, the legal documents will be worthless, but during the preparation and design of the location, everyone should have well-defined legal roles. Buying adjoining properties with individual ownership makes the most sense. Plus, it is a great test of the commitment and dynamics of your group to ensure everyone has some skin in the game.
- Consider conex boxes and shipping containers as buildings. They are cheap and long lasting.
- Good fences make good neighbors. Build a compound that will protect you from a horde of a dozen reanimated rotting corpses.

Once you have your location, stock it with enough of the following supplies to support everyone in your group, for 1 month. Better to have it and not need it, then to need it and not have it.

- Food – 2000 calories per person, per day
- Water – 2 quarts per person, per day
- CB Radio
- Wind-up emergency radio
- Gloves
- Elbow and knee pads
- Helmets
- Safety goggles
- Nose plug
- Appropriate footwear.
- This Zombie Preparedness Guide
- Quality tools that will last a lifetime. Hand tools, yard tools, construction tools, kitchen tools, consider each purchase the last you will have in your lifetime.

The First Days

Plan to be productive during the first days of bugging out. While the ill prepared are chomped into the zombie masses, while the supply chains falter due to mass hysteria, while the interstates fill with abandoned cars, and while the power grid shuts down from the lack of daily maintenance, you will be following your zombie apocalypse preparedness plan by advancing to your prepped bug out location and staying busy.

Before leaving your home and work, cache additional supplies at both. While you may not come back, you will appreciate them being there if you do. Hide them somewhere not easily accessible; like you, the other living will most likely pilfer all they can find.

Dress for the occasion. Wear layers of loose clothing. Hats, long sleeves, pants, long socks, hiking boots, and gloves may all come in handy, even during summer months. Sandals and wife beaters make humorous outfits for the dead warmed over, so, do not be that guy.

For the trip to your prepped bug out location, take all you can comfortably carry.

Once at your bug out site, review your zombie survival plan. Start with your team. Did everyone arrive? Did anyone not make it? Do you have new team members you were not expecting? Can you leverage the differences in team membership such that the unexpected fill the roles of those who did not make it? After assessing your actual zombie survival team's levels of skill and training, remind everyone of the team's expectations for surviving the zombie apocalypse. Start training the newbies.

Even with extensive training, the realization of the actual outbreak may be enough to skew the decision making capabilities of some. This is where teamwork saves the day from the undead. The stronger team members will rise to leadership roles. Leadership should ensure a review of survival tools and provisions. Everyone should be reminded to keep your head where your feet are.

With the team intact, established roles, an overall acceptance of the situation, and a group zombie survival will, you will be more likely to survive the zombie apocalypse.

While these first days should find you with sufficient water, shelter and food, prepare yourself for the future travelling and your long-term retreat.

At some point, your team will make the decision to move. Each time you leave a location, consider leaving a note for others explaining what you left behind, your skills, and where you are going. Would you not, upon arriving at a new bug out location, like to have an assessment of other zombie survivalists?

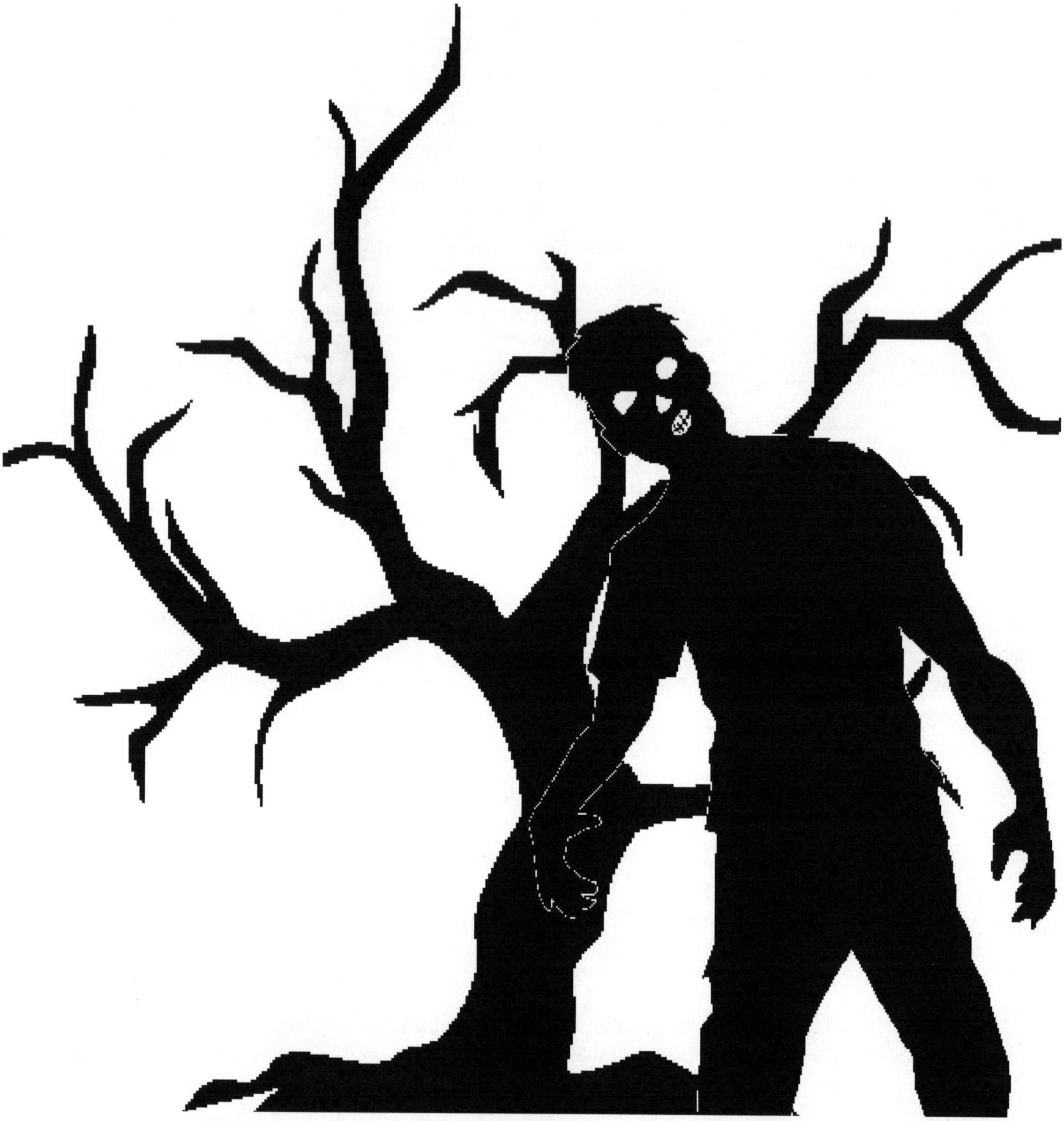

The greatest damage and threat in the first 7 days of the outbreak will come from humans, not the reanimated, as a scramble for control over limited resources, combined with the mass exodus attempts to escape, will represent 90% of the casualties during this period.

People without the skills to farm, fish, prepare food, build shelter, and protect themselves from the elements, while dealing with the reanimated, will be helpless. Skilled laborers, who know how to make things, grow things, and do things will rise from expendable to positions of great value.

The difference between surviving with the living or joining the ranks of the shuffling hungry corpses will be your ability to perform survival actions.

4 - ZOMBIE APOCALYPSE SURVIVAL ACTIONS

The following paragraphs expand on the meaning of each letter of the words ZOMBIE SURVIVAL. Study and remember what each letter signifies because some day you may have to make the words work for you.

Z—Zero In on Surviving

A key ingredient in any zombie survival situation is the mental attitude of the individual involved. Having zombie survival skills is important; having the will to survive the zombie apocalypse is essential. Without a desire to survive the upcoming zombie apocalypse, acquired skills serve little purpose and invaluable knowledge goes to waste. Zero in on the primary goal; surviving the hordes of undead.

O—Overcome Obstacles with Opportunities

Abraham Lincoln wrote, "I will prepare and someday my chance will come." We can only assume he was referring to overcoming obstacles like the reanimated cadavers, turning them into an opportunity to be in a better position through surviving. When the undead infection spreads, there is a 100% guarantee that you will be faced with the associated obstacles – bet on it. How will you react once you are faced with undead tribulations?

You could succumb to the hordes of undead, and just give up trying to survive. Or, you could gain the perspective you had when you chose to read this book. Turn the zombie apocalypse into an opportunity, through a positive perspective, until you achieve the desired outcome.

How you handle obstacles is a choice, and it is no one else's choice but yours. Start today by embracing a zombie survivalist lifestyle. That rapping, rapping at your chamber door could be a zombie, or it may be opportunity knocking.

M—Make Informed Decisions

Informed decisions are decisions where reasoned choices are made by a reasonable individual using information about the pros and cons of the possible courses of action, in accord with the individual's beliefs. Everyone will make life or death decisions during the zombie apocalypse. If you want to survive, make those decisions informed decisions following these steps.

> Step 1. Commit to making decisions through reason, instead of ignorance or irrationality, by replacing emotion with logic.
>
> Step 2. Gather and process information through personal experience and from trusted sources like your reliable zombie survivalist teammates.
>
> Step 3. Weigh the pros and cons of possible courses of action, focusing on actions that would turn obstacles into opportunity, and taking into account your personal beliefs and knowledge of the undead.
>
> Step 4. Choose the best decision, and stick to it until you learn contradictory information or your beliefs change.

Fortunately, making informed decisions need not take hours, as you will need to make some split-second, life or death, decisions. By training yourself during the pre-zombie-apocalyptic environment to follow these four steps, you will be ready when a split-second is the difference between avoiding the undead and becoming the undead.

B—Be Prepared

Preparation means preparing yourself and your zombie survival kit for those contingencies that you have in your plan. A zombie apocalypse survival plan without any preparation is just a piece of paper. It will not keep you among the dwindling ranks of the living. Prepare yourself by making sure your immunizations and dental work are up-to-date. Break in your hiking boots and make sure that the boots have good soles and water-repellent properties. Study the area, climate, terrain, and indigenous sources of food and water. You should continuously assess data, even after the zombie apocalypse survival plan is made, to update the plan as necessary and give you the greatest possible chance of survival. Practice those things that you have planned with the items in your zombie survival kit. Checking ensures that items work and that you know how to use them. Hike five miles and build a fire in the rain so you know that when it is critical to get warm, you can do it. Review the medical items in your kit and have instructions printed on their use so that even in times of stress, you will not make life-threatening errors. Proper planning prevents poor performance.

I—Invest In Your Future

Do not hold back your time and effort during the pre-zombie-apocalyptic world, nor while the hordes of undead are searching the streets for your bug out location. Half-assed planning and preparing for the zombie apocalypse will result in losing half your ass to the mouths of the flesh eating undead.

Both now and then, get up, pay attention, and actively pursue surviving the attack of the reanimated soulless human corpses. It is your life; invest both time and effort in your future.

E—Easy Does It

Especially when operating in a zombie infested environment, burdened with the constant pressure of potentially being attacked and the confusion that goes with dealing with the shuffling undead, our minds turn to the hope of survival. This may tempt us to try too hard to fill needs and get to a long-term survival retreat too quickly. A Hummer would seem to move us around better than walking. The house down the street, with the manual well pump, would ensure regular access to water. Fortifying a grocery store would ensure a lasting food supply. But, with a little patience and forethought, we will find better solutions. Easy does it. Approaching each zombie survival challenge with a relaxed, objective mindset, you will find preferable outcomes.

S—Size Up the Situation

If you are in a situation involving the reanimated, find a place where you can conceal and defend yourself. Remember, security takes priority. Use your senses of hearing, smell, and sight to get a feel for the outbreak. Determine where the flesh eaters are attacking, heading, or gathering. You will have to consider what is developing, regarding the reanimated, when you take the next step towards surviving.

Surroundings

Determine the pattern of the area and outbreak. Get a feel for what is going on around you. Every outbreak environment, whether forest, jungle, or desert, has a rhythm. This tempo includes wildlife and zombie noises, sounds of the elements, and insect sounds. It may also include zombie traffic and other survivalist movements.

Physical Condition

The pressure of your last zombie encounter, or the trauma of being in a zombie situation, may have caused you to overlook wounds you received. Check for wounds regularly. Give yourself first aid, or, if infected, maybe a suicidal blow. Take care to prevent further bodily harm. In any climate, drink plenty of water to prevent dehydration. If you are in a cold or wet climate, put on additional clothing to prevent hypothermia.

Equipment

Perhaps in the heat of zombie panic, you lost or damaged some of your equipment. Check to see what equipment you have and in what condition it is.

Now that you have sized up your situation, surroundings, physical condition, and equipment, you are ready to review, adjust, and continue your zombie survival plan. In doing so, keep in mind your basic physical needs—water, food, shelter, and avoidance of the undead.

U— Undue Haste Makes Waste, Use All Your Senses

You may make a wrong move when you react quickly to zombie presence without thinking or planning. That move may result in unnecessary exposure to zombies, zombie altercations, or death. Do not move just for the sake of taking action. Consider all aspects of your situation before you make a decision and a move. If you act in haste, you may forget or lose some of your equipment. In your haste you may also become disoriented so that you do not know which way to go. Plan your moves. Be ready to move out quickly without endangering yourself. Use all your senses to evaluate the situation. Note zombie sounds (dragging of feet, guttural airflow) and smells (rotten flesh, gaseous releases). Be sensitive to temperature changes. Always be observant.

R—Remember Where You Are

This basic principle is one that you must always follow. If there are other persons with you, make sure they also know their location. Always know who in your group is familiar with the area. If that person is killed by zombies, you will have to build on their last directional statement. Pay close attention to where you are, where you are going, where the infected are, and where they are going. Do not rely on others in the group to keep track of the route. Constantly orient yourself. Always try to determine, as a minimum, how your location relates to the location of—

- Zombies
- Seemingly safe areas
- Other survivalists
- Local water sources (especially important in the desert)
- Areas that will provide good physical safety and concealment

This information will allow you to make intelligent decisions when you are in a zombie apocalypse survival situation.

V—Vanquish Fear and Panic

The greatest enemies when faced with a reanimated rotting corpse are fear and panic. If uncontrolled, they can destroy your ability to make an intelligent decision about the undead. They may cause you to react to your feelings and imagination rather than to your situation. These emotions can drain your energy and thereby cause other negative emotions. Zombie survival training and self-confidence will enable you to vanquish fear and panic.

I—Improvise

In pre-zombie apocalyptic modern life, you have items available for all our needs. Many of these items are cheap to replace when damaged. Our easy-come, easy-go, easy-to-replace culture makes it unnecessary for us to improvise. This inexperience in "making do" can be an enemy in a zombie apocalypse situation. Learn to improvise. Take a tool designed for a specific purpose and see how many other uses you can make of it. Make a game of this during your zombie apocalypse hands-on survival training.

Learn to use natural objects around you for different needs. An example is using a rock for a hammer as you train (using real pig heads) to crush the skulls of the undead. No matter how complete a zombie survival kit you have with you, it will run out or wear out through use. Your imagination must take over when your kit wears out; as the reanimated's persistent aggression will not.

V—Value Living

All of us were born kicking and fighting to live, but we have become accustomed to the easy life. We have become creatures of comfort. We dislike inconveniences like the reality of zombies and discomforts like the potential of being attacked by one. What happens when we are faced with the zombie apocalypse, with its stresses, inconveniences, and discomforts? This is when the will to live—placing a high value on living—is vital. The experience and knowledge you have gained through life and your zombie survival training will have a bearing on your will to live. Stubbornness, a refusal to give in to problems, obstacles, and the infected, will give you the mental and physical strength to endure.

A—Act Like the Locals

The locals and animals of a region have adapted to their environment. To get a feel of the area, watch how the local survivalists go about their daily routine of living and avoiding the stumbling, ravenously hungry corpses. When and what do they eat? When, where, and how do they get their food? When and where do they go for water? What time do they usually go to bed and get up? How do they track and avoid attacks by the shuffling horrors? These actions are important to you when you are trying to avoid zombies.

Animal life in the area can also give you clues on how to survive. Animals also require food, water, and shelter. By watching them, you can find sources of water and food. Keep in mind that the reaction of animals can reveal the presence of zombies.

WARNING: Animals cannot serve as an absolute guide to what you can eat and drink. Many animals eat plants that are toxic to humans.

WARNING: Many animals also show a general disregard for zombies; not a healthy attitude for a survivalist.

If you find yourself in a seemingly zombie free area, one way you can gain rapport with the locals is to show interest in their survival and how they get food and water. By studying the other living, you learn to respect them, you often make valuable friends, and, most important, you learn how to adapt to their environment and increase your chances of surviving the zombie apocalypse.

L—Live by Your Wits, *But for Now,* Learn Basic Skills

Without training in basic skills for surviving and avoiding the undead, your chances of living through a zombie situation are slight.

Learn these basic skills **now**—not when you are headed for, or are surrounded by, the flesh-hungry undead. How you decide to equip yourself before the outbreak will affect whether or not you survive the flesh eating hordes. You need to know about the environment to which you are going, and you must practice basic skills geared to that environment. For instance, if you are going to a desert, you need to know how to get water.

Practice basic zombie survival skills during all training programs and exercises. Zombie survival training reduces fear of the unknown and gives you self-confidence. It teaches you to live by your wits.

PATTERN FOR ZOMBIE SURVIVAL

Develop a zombie survival pattern that lets you beat the undead. This zombie survival pattern must include food, water, shelter, fire, first aid, and avoiding zombies, placed in order of importance. For example, in a cold environment, you would need a **fire** to get warm; a **shelter** to protect you from the zombies, cold, wind, and rain or snow; traps or snares to get **food**; and **first aid** to maintain health. If you are injured, first aid has second priority, only after dealing with immediate zombie threats, no matter the climate.

Change your zombie survival pattern to meet your immediate physical needs as the environment changes. As you learn from the rest of this zombie apocalypse survival guide, keep in mind the keywords ZOMBIE SURVIVAL, what each letter signifies, and the need for a zombie survival pattern.

Z	Zero In On Surviving
O	Overcome Obstacles With Opportunities
M	Make Informed Decisions
B	Be Prepared
I	Invest in Your Future
E	Easy Does It

S	Size Up the Situation (Surroundings, Physical Condition, Equipment)
U	Undue Haste Makes Waste, Use All Your Senses
R	Remember Where You Are
V	Vanquish Fear and Panic
I	Improvise
V	Value Living
A	Act Like the Natives
L	Live by Your Wits, but for now, Learn Basic Skills

The following medical procedures are only for survival use during the zombie apocalypse. Before the outbreak, always seek professional medical assistance. The sooner you heal, the more likely you will be ready when the undead arrive.

Not all of us are doctors, so during the zombie apocalypse, we will likely find ourselves in the very traumatic situation of having to deal with injuries and illnesses beyond our knowledge and abilities. More than anything, this chapter should help us identify our lack of skill and prompt us to invest in training.

Right now, *call your closest CNA, EMT, First Responder, Nurse, Doctor, or medical professional friend to form an alliance to fill the medical position on your zombie apocalypse survival team.*

5 - MEDICAL

INFECTED?

Any sign of the injured being infected, scratched, or bitten is a prompt to handle them as a potential undead threat. Access the condition as a potential zombie infection and treat as necessary.

The first question we have to ask is, "Is this injury the result of direct contact with the infected?" If so, step away and refer to the injured's previously expressed will regarding the handling of them as a zombie. Infection set-in rates vary individual by individual, so do not expect you will have enough time for long goodbyes. Watch for telltale signs of infection like cuts oozing something other than blood, discoloration of the eyes, excessive muscle twitches, gnarling of the teeth, or a conspicuous lack of breathing. If the injured is responsive, ask them for signs if they feel they are becoming infected. If you can, stay with them, but do not allow yourself to become infected. At the first sign of infection, if you are not already far enough away, and the injured previously requested a mercy killing, kill them. If the injured is unresponsive, excellent, destroy the brain quickly allowing them a fast and painless death.

They may have been a good person, but the only good zombie is a dead zombie.

NOT INFECTED?

Foremost among the many problems that can compromise your zombie survivability are medical problems resulting from unplanned events.

Many survivors of zombie outbreaks report difficulty in treating injuries and illness due to the lack of training and medical supplies. For the less fortunate, this leads to succumbing to the dead warmed over.

Survivors of zombie outbreaks have related feelings of apathy and helplessness because they could not treat themselves, nor others, in this environment. The ability to treat yourself medically increases your morale and aids in your personal and team survival.

One survivor with a fair amount of basic medical knowledge can make a difference in the lives of many. Without qualified medical personnel available, it is you who must know what to do to stay alive.

REQUIREMENTS FOR MAINTENANCE OF HEALTH

To survive, you need **water** and **food**. Unlike the stinky undead hordes, you must also have and apply **high personal hygiene** standards.

WATER

Your body loses water through normal bodily processes (sweating, urinating, and defecating). During average daily exertion, the average adult loses, and therefore requires, 2 to 3 liters of water. Other factors, such as heat exposure, cold exposure, intense activity like running from the reanimated, high altitude, burns, fear, or illness, can cause your body to lose more water. You must replace this water.

Dehydration results from inadequate replacement of lost bodily fluids. It decreases your efficiency to deal with the stumbling, ravenously hungry corpses and, if you are injured, it increases your susceptibility to severe shock and death at the hands of the shuffling horrors.

Consider the following results of bodily fluid loss:

- A 5-percent loss results in thirst, irritability, nausea, and weakness.
- A 10-percent loss results in dizziness, headache, inability to walk, and a tingling sensation in the limbs.
- A 15-percent loss results in dim vision, painful urination, swollen tongue, deafness, and a numb feeling in the skin.
- If your weakness hasn't already resulted in your succumbing to the undead, a loss greater than 15 percent may result in death.

The most common signs and symptoms of dehydration are—

- Dark urine with a very strong odor
- Low urine output
- Dark, sunken eyes
- Fatigue
- Emotional instability
- Trench line down center of tongue
- Thirst

You should replace water as you lose it. Trying to make up a deficit is difficult in a zombie survival situation, and thirst is not a sign of how much water you need. Most people cannot comfortably drink more than 1 liter of water at a time. So, even when not thirsty, drink small amounts of water at regular intervals each hour to prevent dehydration.

One alternate method through which hydration can be achieved is through the rectal route. Fluids do not need to be sterile, only purified. One can effectively absorb approximately 1 to 1.5 liters per hour by using a tube to deliver fluids into the rectal vault.

Of all the physical problems encountered in a flesh eating rotting corpse situation, the loss of water is the most preventable. The following are basic guidelines for the prevention of dehydration:

- *Always drink water when eating.* Water is used and consumed as a part of the digestion process and can lead to dehydration.
- *Acclimatize.* The body performs more efficiently in extreme conditions when acclimatized.
- *Conserve sweat, not water.* Limit sweat-producing activities but drink water.

Because you will be under the physical and mental stress of dealing with the reanimated, increase your water intake. Another chapter will delve into more detail regarding water.

FOOD

If you are not too actively running from the undead, although you can live several weeks without food, you need an adequate amount to stay healthy. Without food your mental and physical capabilities will deteriorate rapidly and you fall to the zombies. Food provides energy and replenishes the substances that your body burns. Food provides vitamins, minerals, salts, and other elements essential to good health. Possibly more important, it helps morale.

The three basic sources of food are plants, animals (including fish), and prepped rations. In varying degrees, all provide the calories, carbohydrates, fats, and proteins needed for normal daily body functions. You should use prepped rations to augment plant and animal foods, which will extend and help maintain a balanced diet.

Calories are a measure of heat and potential energy. The average person needs 2,000 calories per day to function at a minimum level. An adequate amount of carbohydrates, fats, and proteins without an adequate caloric intake will lead to starvation and cannibalism of the body's own tissue for energy. And you thought the zombies were the only cannibalistic concern!

Plants

Plant foods provide carbohydrates—the main source of energy. Many plants provide enough protein to keep the body at normal efficiency. Although plants may not provide a balanced diet, they will sustain you even in the arctic, where meat's heat-producing qualities are normally essential and the reanimated freeze to immobility. Many plant foods such as nuts and seeds will give you enough protein and oils for normal efficiency. Roots, green vegetables, and plant foods containing natural sugar will provide calories and carbohydrates that give the body natural energy.

The food value of plants becomes more important if you are eluding the shuffling hordes or if you are in an area where wildlife is scarce. For instance—

- You can dry plants by wind, air, sun, or fire. This retards spoilage so that you can store or carry the plant food with you to use when needed.
- You can obtain plants more easily and more quietly than meat. This is extremely important when trying to avoid the attention of the undead.

Animals

Meat is more nourishing than plant food. In fact, it may even be more readily available in some places. However, to get meat, you need to know the habits of, and how to capture, various wildlife.

To satisfy your immediate food needs, first seek the more abundant and more easily obtained wildlife, such as insects, crustaceans, mollusks, fish, and reptiles. These can satisfy your immediate hunger while you are preparing traps and snares for larger game.

Another chapter will delve into more detail regarding food.

PERSONAL HYGIENE

Cleanliness is an important factor in preventing infection and disease. It becomes even more important in a zombie survival situation. Poor hygiene can reduce your chances of surviving the undead.

A daily shower with hot water and soap is ideal, but you can stay clean without this luxury. Use a cloth and soapy water to wash yourself. Pay special attention to the feet, armpits, crotch, hands, and hair as these are prime areas for infestation and infection. If water is scarce, take an "air" bath. Be sure there are no zombies in the area, then remove as much of your clothing as practical and expose your body to the sun and air for at least 1 hour. Be careful not to sunburn.

If you do not have soap, use ashes or sand, or make soap from animal fat and hardwood ashes if your situation allows. To make soap—

- Extract grease from animal fat by cutting the fat into small pieces and cooking it in a pot.
- Add enough water to the pot to keep the fat from sticking as it cooks.
- Cook the fat slowly, stirring frequently, until the fat is rendered into a liquid.

- Place hardwood ashes in a container with a spout near the bottom.
- Pour water over the ashes and collect the liquid that drips out of the spout in a separate container. This liquid is the potash or lye.

- Mix the lye and grease while the grease is still liquid.

After the mixture (the soap) cools, you can use it in the semiliquid state directly from the pot. You can also pour it into a pan, allow it to harden, and cut it into bars for later use.

Keep Your Hands Clean

Germs on your hands can infect food and wounds. Wash your hands after handling any material that is likely to have come in contact with zombified flesh or carry germs, after urinating or defecating, after caring for the sick, and before handling any food, food utensils, or drinking water. Keep your fingernails closely trimmed and clean, and keep your fingers out of your mouth.

Keep Your Hair Clean

Your hair can become a haven for bacteria or fleas, lice, and other parasites. Keeping your hair clean, combed, and trimmed helps you avoid this danger. Short hair is easier to keep clean and less apt to be entangled in obstacles or grabbed by the undead.

Keep Your Clothing Clean

Keep your clothing and bedding as clean as possible to reduce the chances of skin infection or parasitic infestation. Never sleep in an area that has been populated by zombies. Clean your outer clothing whenever it becomes soiled. Wear clean underclothing and socks each day. If water is scarce, "air" clean your clothing by shaking, airing, and sunning it for 2 hours. If you are using a sleeping bag, turn it inside out after each use, fluff it, and air it.

Keep Your Teeth Clean

Thoroughly clean your mouth and teeth with a toothbrush at least once each day. If you do not have a toothbrush, make one by chewing one end of a small stick to separate the fibers. Then brush your teeth thoroughly. Rinse with water or salt water. Flossing with string or fiber helps oral hygiene.

Take Care of Your Feet

Your feet will be two of your greatest assets during a zombie outbreak. To prevent serious foot problems, break in your shoes before wearing them during the outbreak. Wash and massage your feet daily. Trim your toenails straight across. Check your feet daily for blisters.

If you get a small blister, do not open it. An intact blister is safe from infection. Apply a padding material around the blister to relieve pressure and reduce friction. If the blister bursts, treat it as an open wound; watch for signs of zombism. Clean and dress it daily and pad around it. Leave large blisters intact.

Keep Bug Out Locations Clean

Do not soil the ground in the bug out area with urine or feces. When bathrooms are not available, dig "cat holes" and cover the waste. Collect drinking water upstream from the bug out location. Purify all water.

Get Sufficient Rest When You Can

Even though the undead will never-endingly hunt you, you need a certain amount of rest to keep going. During your daily activities, plan for regular rest periods of at least 10 minutes per hour. Learn to make yourself comfortable under the flesh eating infested, less-than-ideal conditions. A change from mental to physical activity or vice versa can be refreshing when time or situation does not permit total relaxation.

MEDICAL EMERGENCIES

Medical problems and emergencies you may face during the zombie apocalypse include breathing problems, severe bleeding, and shock. The following paragraphs explain each of these problems and what you can expect if they occur.

Breathing Problems

Any one of the following can cause airway obstruction, resulting in stopped breathing:

- Fear of zombies or the horrors of the zombie apocalypse.
- Foreign matter in mouth or throat that obstructs the opening to the trachea.
- Face or neck injuries.
- The tongue can block passage of air to the lungs upon unconsciousness. When an individual is unconscious, the muscles of the lower jaw and tongue relax as the neck drops forward, causing the lower jaw to sag and the tongue to drop back and block the passage of air.

Severe Bleeding

Severe bleeding from any major blood vessel in the body is extremely dangerous. The loss of 1 liter of blood will produce moderate symptoms of shock. The loss of 2 liters will produce a severe state of shock that places the body in extreme danger. The loss of any more than 2 liters is usually fatal during the terrors and limited medical resources of zombie outbreaks.

Shock

Shock is a clinical condition characterized by symptoms that arise when cardiac output is insufficient to fill the arteries with blood under enough pressure to provide an adequate blood supply to the organs and tissues. Next to zombie attacks, shock is the second most likely injury leading to death during zombie outbreaks.

LIFESAVING STEPS

Follow the ABCs (Airway, Breathing, and Circulation) of first aid. Perform a rapid physical exam. Look for the cause of the injury and start with the airway and breathing, but be discerning. In some cases, a person may die from arterial bleeding more quickly than from an airway obstruction. Always be on the lookout for signs of zombism. The following paragraphs describe how to treat airway, bleeding, and shock emergencies.

Airway and Breathing

If the victim is conscious, or actively working to clear their own airway, let them work it out themselves. Provide, at the, most the Heimlich maneuver. Control panic, both your own and the victim's. Be reassuring and try to keep them quiet to avoid being detected by the undead.

If the victim is unconscious and not breathing, you can try to open an airway and maintain breathing by using the following steps:

Airway Step 1. Check to see if the victim has a partial or complete airway obstruction. If they can cough, allow them to clear the obstruction naturally. If their airway is completely obstructed, administer abdominal thrusts (Heimlich) until the obstruction is cleared.

Airway Step 2. After ensuring the victim is not a zombie concern, if you can see an obstruction, using a finger, quickly sweep the victim's mouth clear of foreign objects like broken teeth, etc.

Breathing Step 3. With the victim's airway open, pinch their nose closed with your thumb and forefinger and blow two complete breaths into their lungs. Allow the lungs to deflate after the second inflation and perform the following:

- **Look** for their chest to rise and fall.
- **Listen** for escaping air during exhalation. Expect it to sound like the undead.
- **Feel** for flow of air on your cheek.

Breathing Step 4. If the forced breaths do not stimulate spontaneous breathing, watch for signs of zombism and maintain the victim's breathing by performing mouth-to-mouth resuscitation.

Breathing Step 5. Sometimes victims vomit during mouth-to-mouth resuscitation. Clear as needed.

NOTE: Cardiopulmonary resuscitation (CPR) may be necessary after cleaning the airway, but only after major bleeding is under control. Learn CPR **before** the zombie apocalypse.

CONTROL BLEEDING

In an undead survival situation, you must control serious bleeding immediately because replacement fluids normally are not available and the victim can die within a matter of minutes. You can control external bleeding by direct pressure, indirect (pressure points) pressure, elevation, digital ligation, or tourniquet. Each method is explained below.

Direct Pressure

The most effective way to control external bleeding is by applying pressure directly over the wound. This pressure must not only be firm enough to stop the bleeding, but it must also be maintained long enough to "seal off" the damaged surface.

If bleeding continues after having applied direct pressure for 30 minutes, apply a pressure dressing. This dressing consists of a thick dressing of gauze or other suitable material applied directly over the wound and held in place with a tightly wrapped bandage. It should be tighter than an ordinary compression bandage but not so tight that it impairs circulation to the rest of the limb. Once you apply the dressing, **do not remove it,** even when the dressing becomes blood soaked. Constantly monitor the victim for signs of zombism.

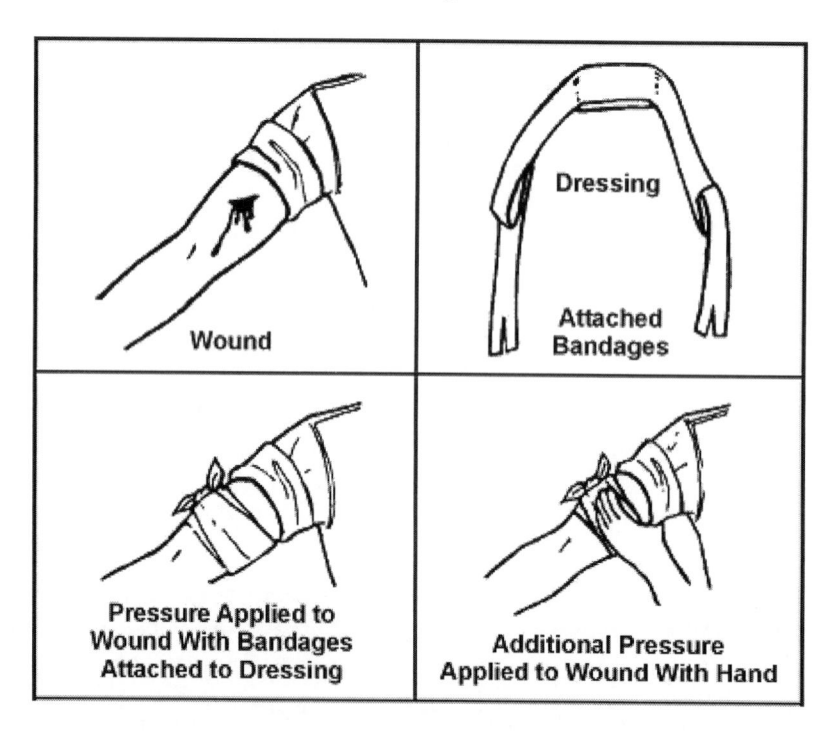

Wound	Dressing / Attached Bandages
Pressure Applied to Wound With Bandages Attached to Dressing	Additional Pressure Applied to Wound With Hand

Leave the pressure dressing in place for 1 or 2 days, after which you can remove and replace it with a smaller dressing. To promote long-term survival in a zombie infested environment, make fresh, daily dressing changes and inspect for signs of infection.

Elevation

Raising an injured extremity as high as possible above the heart's level slows blood loss by aiding the return of blood to the heart and lowering the blood pressure at the wound. However, elevation alone will not control bleeding entirely; you must also apply direct pressure over the wound.

Pressure Points

A pressure point is a location where the main artery to the wound lies near the surface of the skin or where the artery passes directly over a bony prominence.

You can use digital pressure on a pressure point to slow arterial bleeding until the application of a pressure dressing. Pressure point control is not as effective for controlling bleeding as direct pressure exerted on the wound.

Regarding pressure points, follow this rule: Apply pressure at the end of the joint just above the injured area. On hands, feet, and head, this will be the wrist, ankle, and neck, respectively.

> **WARNING**
>
> Use caution when applying pressure to the neck. Too much pressure for too long may cause unconsciousness or death. Never place a tourniquet around the neck.

Maintain pressure points by placing a round stick in the joint, bending the joint over the stick, and then keeping it tightly bent by lashing. By using this method to maintain pressure, it frees your hands to work in other areas.

When treating a zombie bite, use the pressure of a knife through the brain of the victim; it is less resource costly than ammunition.

Finger Pinch

You can stop major bleeding immediately or slow it down by applying pressure with a finger or two on the bleeding end of the vein or artery. Maintain the pressure until the risk of imminent zombie attack, or until the bleeding stops or slows down enough to apply a pressure bandage, elevation, and so forth.

Tourniquet

Use a tourniquet only when direct pressure over the bleeding point and all other methods did not control the bleeding. If you leave a tourniquet in place too long, the damage to the tissues can progress to gangrene, with a loss of the limb later, and eventual death. An improperly applied tourniquet can also cause permanent damage to nerves and other tissues at the site of the constriction. If you must use a tourniquet, place it around the extremity, between the wound and the heart, 2 to 4 inches above the wound site. Never place it directly over the wound or a fracture.

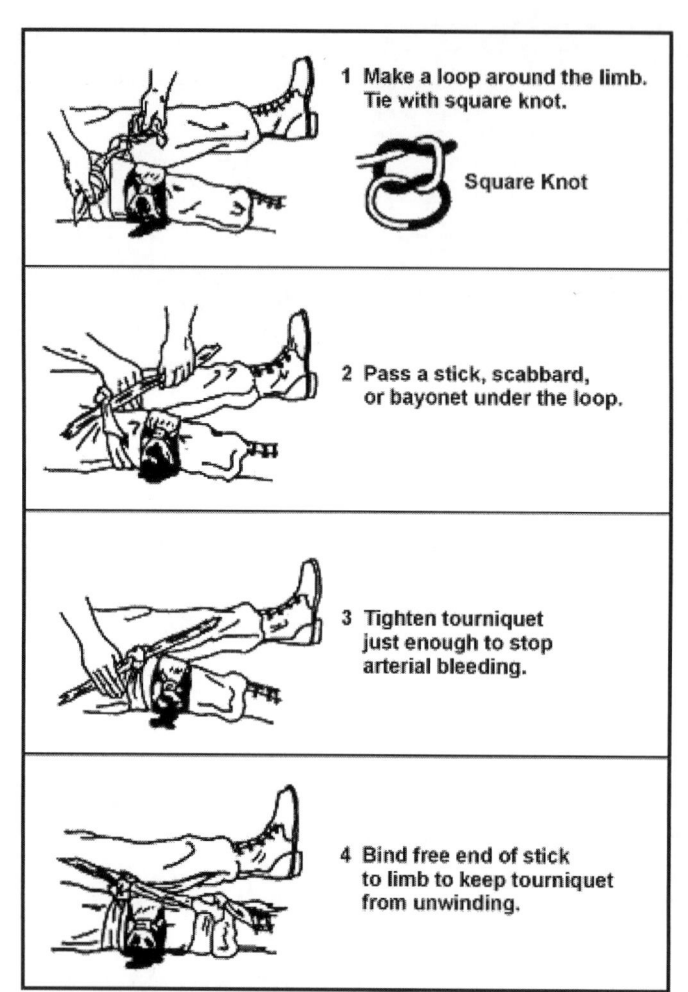

1. Make a loop around the limb. Tie with square knot.
2. Pass a stick, scabbard, or bayonet under the loop.
3. Tighten tourniquet just enough to stop arterial bleeding.
4. Bind free end of stick to limb to keep tourniquet from unwinding.

After you secure the tourniquet, inspect for signs of zombism, then clean and bandage the wound. A lone zombie survivalist **should not** remove or release an applied tourniquet. However, in a buddy system, the buddy can release the tourniquet pressure every 10 to 15 minutes for 1 or 2 minutes to let blood flow to the rest of the extremity to prevent limb loss.

PREVENT AND TREAT SHOCK

Anticipate shock in all injured personnel. Unless there are signs of zombism, treat all injured persons as follows, regardless of what symptoms appear:

- If the victim is conscious, place them on a level surface with the lower extremities elevated 6 to 8 inches.

- If the victim is unconscious, place them on their side or abdomen with their head turned to one side to prevent choking on vomit, blood, or other fluids.

- If you are unsure of the best position, place the victim perfectly flat. Once the victim is in a shock position, do not move them unless there is an imminent zombie attack.

- Maintain body heat by insulating the victim from the surroundings and, in some instances, applying external heat.

- If wet, remove all the victim's wet clothing as soon as possible and replace with dry clothing.

- Improvise a shelter to insulate the victim from the weather and hide from the undead.

- Use warm liquids or foods, a pre-warmed sleeping bag, another person, warmed water in canteens, hot rocks wrapped in clothing, or fires on either side of the victim to provide external warmth.

- If the victim is conscious, slowly administer small doses of a warm salt or sugar solution.

- If the victim is unconscious or has abdominal wounds, do not give fluids by mouth.

- If the shuffling hordes will let you, have the victim rest for at least 24 hours.

- If you are a lone zombie survivalist, lie in a depression in the ground, behind a tree, or any other place out of the weather and away from the flesh eaters, with your head lower than your feet.

- If you are with a buddy, reassess your patient constantly.

BONE AND JOINT INJURY

While surviving the zombie apocalypse, you will likely face bone and joint injuries that include fractures, dislocations, and sprains. Follow the steps explained below for each injury.

Fractures

The two types of fractures are open and closed. With an open (or compound) fracture, the bone protrudes through the skin and complicates the actual fracture with an open wound. Any bone protruding from the wound should be cleaned with an antiseptic and kept moist. You should splint the injured area and continually monitor blood flow past the injury. Only reposition the break if there is no blood flow. <u>Only in the best of zombie apocalyptic scenarios is this not the kiss of death; prioritize your resources appropriately</u>.

The closed fracture has no open wounds. Follow the guidelines for immobilization and splint the fracture.

The signs and symptoms of a fracture are pain, tenderness, discoloration, swelling deformity, loss of function, and grating (a sound or feeling that occurs when broken bone ends rub together).

The dangers with a fracture are the severing or the compression of a nerve or blood vessel at the site of fracture. For this reason minimum manipulation should be done, and only very cautiously. If you notice the area below the break becoming numb, swollen, cool to the touch, or turning pale, and the victim showing signs of shock, a major vessel may have been severed. You must control this internal bleeding. Reset the fracture and treat the victim for shock and replace lost fluids. <u>Only in the best of zombie apocalyptic scenarios is this not the kiss of death; prioritize your resources appropriately</u>.

Often you must maintain traction during the splinting and healing process. You can effectively pull smaller bones such as the arm or lower leg by hand. You can then splint the break.

Very strong muscles hold a broken thighbone (femur) in place making it difficult to maintain traction during healing. <u>As such, only in the best of zombie apocalyptic scenarios is this not the kiss of death; prioritize your resources appropriately</u>.

Dislocations

Dislocations are the separations of bone joints causing the bones to go out of proper alignment. These misalignments can be extremely painful and can cause an impairment of nerve or circulatory function below the affected area. You must place these joints back into alignment as quickly as possible.

Signs and symptoms of dislocations are joint pain, tenderness, swelling, discoloration, limited range of motion, and deformity of the joint. Treat dislocations by reduction, immobilization, and rehabilitation.

Reduction or "setting" is placing the bones back into their proper alignment. You can use several methods, but manual traction or the use of weights to pull the bones are the safest and easiest. Once performed, reduction decreases the victim's pain and allows for normal function and circulation. Because, during the zombie apocalypse, you probably will not have access to an X ray machine, you can judge proper alignment by the look and feel of the joint and by comparing it to the joint on the opposite side.

Immobilization is nothing more than splinting the dislocation after reduction. You can use any cloth material for a splint, and you can splint an extremity to the body. The basic guidelines for splinting are as follows:

- Splint above and below the fracture site.
- Pad splints to reduce discomfort.
- Check circulation below the fracture after making each tie on the splint.

To rehabilitate the dislocation, remove the splints after 7 to 14 days.

Sprains

Overstretching a tendon or ligament causes sprains. The signs and symptoms are pain, swelling, tenderness, and discoloration (black and blue).

When treating sprains, you should follow the letters in RICE as defined below:

- **R** - Rest injured area.
- **I** - Ice for 24 to 48 hours. Ice is preferred for a sprain but cold spring water may be more easily obtained in a zombie survival situation.
- **C** - Compression-wrap or splint to help stabilize. If possible, leave the boot on a sprained ankle unless circulation is compromised.
- **E** - Elevate the affected area.

BITES (OTHER THAN FROM A ZOMBIE) AND STINGS

Insects and related pests are hazards, even in an undead survival situation. They not only cause irritations, but they are often carriers of diseases that cause severe allergic reactions in some individuals. In many parts of the world they expose serious, even fatal, diseases.

- Ticks can carry and transmit diseases, such as Rocky Mountain spotted fever common in many parts of the United States. Ticks also transmit Lyme disease.
- Mosquitoes may carry malaria, the West Nile virus, and many other diseases.
- Flies can spread disease from contact with infectious sources. They are causes of sleeping sickness, typhoid, cholera, and dysentery.
- Fleas can transmit plague.
- Lice can transmit typhus and relapsing fever.
- As of this publication, there are no documented cases of pests spreading zombism.

If you are bitten (by something other than a flesh eating corpse) or stung, do not scratch the bite or sting; it might become infected. Inspect your body at least once a day to ensure there are no attached insects. If you find ticks attached to your body, cover them with a substance (such as petroleum jelly, heavy oil, or tree sap) that will cut off their air supply. Without air, the tick releases its hold, and you can remove it. Take care to remove the whole tick. Use tweezers if you have them. Grasp the tick where the mouthparts are attached to the skin. Do not squeeze the tick's body. Wash your hands after touching the tick. Clean the tick wound daily until healed.

Treatment

It is impossible to list the treatment of all the different types of bites and stings. However, you can generally treat bites and stings as follows:

- If antibiotics are available, become familiar with them before the outbreak and use them.
- Pre-zombie-apocalyptic immunizations can prevent most of the common diseases carried by mosquitoes and some carried by flies.
- The common fly-borne diseases are usually treatable with penicillin or erythromycin.
- Most tick-, flea-, louse-, and mite-borne diseases are treatable with tetracycline.
- If you are lucky enough to find a pharmacy that hasn't been completely looted, most antibiotics come in 250 milligram (mg) or 500 mg tablets. If you cannot remember the exact dose rate to treat a disease, 2 tablets, 4 times a day, for 10 to 14 days will usually kill any bacteria.

Relieve the itching and discomfort caused by insect bites by applying—

- Cold compresses
- A cooling paste of mud and ashes
- Sap from dandelions
- Coconut meat
- Crushed cloves of garlic
- Onion

Spider Bites And Scorpion Stings

- The black widow spider is identified by a red hourglass on its abdomen.
- The funnel web spider is a large brown or gray spider found in Australia.
- Tarantulas are large, hairy spiders found mainly in the tropics. Most do not inject venom, but some South American species do. If bitten, pain and bleeding are certain, and infection is likely.
- All scorpions are venomous.

The initial pain from bites or stings by these is not severe, but gradually spreads over the entire body and settles in the abdomen and legs making the victim wish they were as numb as the undead. Symptoms may worsen for the next three days and then begin to subside for the next week. Treat for shock. Be ready to perform CPR. Clean and dress the bite area to reduce the risk of infection. Remember to use your resources wisely; in an environment of regular attacks by the shuffling hordes, this victim may not be worth the attention.

The brown recluse spider is a small, light brown spider identified by a dark brown violin on its back. There is so little pain, that usually a victim is not aware of the bite. Within a few hours a painful red area with a splotchy blue center appears. Usually, in 3 to 4 days, a star-shaped, firm area of deep purple discoloration appears at the bite site. The area turns dark and mummified in a week or two. The margins separate and the scab falls off, leaving an open ulcer. The outstanding characteristic of the brown recluse bite is an ulcer that does not heal but persists for weeks or months.

Snakebites

The chance of snakebite in a zombie survival situation is rather small, if you are familiar with the various types of snakes and their habitats. More than one-half of snakebite victims have little or no effects of venom, and only about one-quarter develop into serious injury.

A bite wound, regardless of the type of animal that inflicted it, can become infected from bacteria in the animal's mouth. With nonvenomous as well as venomous snakebites, this local infection is responsible for a large part of the residual damage that results.

Before treating snakebite, determine whether the snake was venomous or nonvenomous. Bites from a nonvenomous snake will show rows of teeth. Bites from a venomous snake may have rows of teeth showing, but will have one or more distinctive puncture marks caused by fang penetration. Symptoms of a venomous bite may be spontaneous bleeding from the nose and anus, blood in the urine, pain and swelling at the site of the bite.

Breathing difficulty, paralysis, weakness, twitching, and numbness are also signs of neurotoxic venoms. These signs usually appear 1.5 to 2 hours after the bite.

If you determine that a venomous snake bit an individual, take the following steps:

- Reassure the victim and keep them still.
- Remove watches, rings, bracelets, or other constricting items.
- Clean the bite area.
- Maintain an airway (especially if bitten near the face or neck).
- Use a constricting band between the wound and the heart.
- Immobilize the site.

Remember five very important guidelines during the treatment of snakebites.

- **Do not** misuse all your medical resources unwisely; in an environment of high zombie threat, this victim may not be worth the resources.
- **Do not** give the victim alcoholic beverages or tobacco products.
- **Do not** make any deep cuts at the bite site. Cutting opens capillaries that in turn open a direct route into the blood stream for venom and infection.
- **Do not** put your hands on your face or rub your eyes, as venom may be on your hands. Venom may cause blindness.
- **Do not** break open the large blisters that form around the bite site.

After caring for the victim as described above, take the following actions to minimize local effects:

- If infection appears, keep the wound open and clean.
- Use heat after 24 to 48 hours to help prevent the spread of local infection. Heat also helps to draw out an infection.
- Keep the wound covered with a dry, sterile dressing.
- Have the victim drink large amounts of fluids until the infection is gone.

WOUNDS

An interruption of the skin's integrity characterizes wounds. These wounds could be open wounds, skin diseases, frostbite, trench foot, or burns. The most important thing to remember is to determine if the wounds were zombie inflicted, or may be zombie infected.

Open Wounds

Open wounds are serious in an undead survival situation, not only because of tissue damage and blood loss, but primarily because they may become infected by zombism. Bacteria may cause infection. If bacteria are from a zombie's wound, zombism is guaranteed; prioritize your resources appropriately.

Taking proper care of the wound you can reduce further contamination and promote healing. Clean the wound as soon as possible after it occurs by—

- Removing or cutting clothing away from the wound.
- Looking for an exit wound if a sharp object, gunshot, or projectile caused a wound.
- Thoroughly cleaning the skin around the wound.
- Rinsing (not scrubbing) the wound with large amounts of water under pressure. You can use fresh urine if water is not available.

The "open treatment" method is the safest way to manage wounds in zombie survival situations. Do not try to close any wound by suturing or similar procedures. Leave the wound open to allow the drainage of any pus resulting from infection. As long as the wound can drain, it generally will not become life-threatening, regardless of how unpleasant it looks or smells.

Cover the wound with a clean dressing. Place a bandage on the dressing to hold it in place. Change the dressing daily to check for zombism or infection.

If a wound is gaping, you can bring the edges together with adhesive tape cut in the form of a "butterfly" or "dumbbell". Use this method with extreme caution in the absence of antibiotics. You must always allow for proper drainage of the wound to avoid infection.

Another way to bring the edges of wounds together is glue. When using glue:

- Only use on "clean" wounds, wounds with straight edges.
- Do not use on profound wounds. Glue on deep wounds can hinder healing.
- Do not use on wounds that still have considerable bleeding.
- Do not use on punctures, bites, infected areas, nor ulcers.
- Super glue is tough to use, use skin-glue, if available, instead.

In a high activity zombie survival situation, some degree of wound infection is almost inevitable. Pain, swelling, and redness around the wound, increased temperature, and pus in the wound or on the dressing indicate infection is present.

Except in the case of zombism, if the wound becomes infected, you should treat as follows:

- Place a warm, moist compress directly on the infected wound. Change the compress when it cools, keeping a warm compress on the wound for a total of 30 minutes. Apply the compresses three or four times daily.
- Drain the wound. Open and gently probe the infected wound with a sterile instrument.
- Dress and bandage the wound.
- Drink a lot of water.
- In the event of gunshot or other serious wounds, it may be better to rinse the wound out vigorously every day with the cleanest water available. If drinking water, or methods to purify drinking water, are limited, do not use your drinking water. Flush the wound forcefully daily until the wound is healed over.
- Continue this treatment daily until all signs of infection have disappeared.

If you do not have antibiotics and the wound has become severely infected, does not heal, and ordinary debridement is impossible, consider maggot therapy as stated below, despite its hazards:

- Expose the wound to flies for one day and then cover it.
- Check the wound every 4 hours for signs of zombism and maggots.
- Once maggots develop, keep wound covered but check daily.
- Remove all maggots when they have cleaned out all dead tissue and before they start on healthy tissue. Increased pain and bright red blood in the wound indicate that the maggots have reached healthy tissue.

- Flush the wound repeatedly with sterile water or fresh urine to remove the maggots.
- Check the wound every 4 hours for several days to ensure all maggots have been removed.
- Bandage the wound and treat it as any other wound. It should heal normally.

<u>If the wound is zombie inflicted, zombism is highly likely; prioritize your resources appropriately.</u>

SKIN DISEASES AND AILMENTS

Even during the zombie apocalypse, boils, fungal infections, and rashes will rarely develop into a serious health problem. There are no documented cases of boils, fungal infections, or rashes developing into zombism. But, they will cause discomfort and you should treat them as follows:

Boils

Apply warm compresses to bring the boil to a head. Another method that can be used to bring a boil to a head is the bottle suction method. Use an empty bottle that has been boiled in water. Place the opening of the bottle over the boil and seal the skin forming an airtight environment that will create a vacuum. This method will draw the pus to the skin surface when applied correctly. Then open the boil using a sterile knife, wire, needle, or similar item. Using soap and water, thoroughly clean out the pus. Cover the boil site, checking it periodically to ensure no further infection develops. Watch for zombism.

Fungal Infections

Keep the skin clean and dry, and expose the infected area to as much sunlight as possible. **Do not scratch** the affected area.

Rashes

To treat a skin rash effectively, observe the following rules:

- If it is moist, keep it dry.
- If it is dry, keep it moist.
- Do not scratch it.
- Treat rashes as open wounds; clean and dress them daily.

BURNS

The following treatment for burns relieves the pain somewhat, seems to help speed healing, and offers some protection against infection (other than zombism):

- Soak dressings or clean rags for 10 minutes in a boiling tannic acid solution (obtained from tea, inner bark of hardwood trees, or acorns boiled in water).
- Cool the dressings or clean rags and apply over burns. Sugar and honey also work for burns with honey being especially effective at promoting new skin growth and stopping infections.
- Treat as an open wound.
- Replace fluid loss. Fluid replacement can be achieved through oral, intravenous (on the rare occasion that resources are available during the zombie apocalypse), or rectal routes.
- If available, consider using morphine, unless the burns are near the face.

ENVIRONMENTAL INJURIES

Heatstroke, hypothermia, diarrhea, and intestinal parasites are environmental injuries you could face in a zombie apocalyptic survival situation. Read and follow the guidance provided below.

Heatstroke

The breakdown of the body's heat regulatory system (body temperature more than 105 degrees F) causes a heatstroke. Signs and symptoms of heatstroke are—

- Swollen, beet-red face
- Reddened whites of eyes
- Victim not sweating
- Unconsciousness or delirium, which can cause pale skin, a bluish color to lips and nail beds, and cool skin

NOTE: By this time, the victim is in severe shock. Cool the victim as rapidly as possible. Cool them by dipping them in a cool stream. If one is not available, douse the victim with urine, water, or at the very least, apply cool wet compresses to all the joints, especially the neck, armpits, and crotch. Be sure to wet the victim's head. Heat loss through the scalp is great. Administer IVs (when available) and provide drinking fluids. Zombie interference aside, you may fan the individual.

You can expect the following symptoms during cooling:

- Vomiting
- Diarrhea
- Shivering
- Shouting
- Prolonged unconsciousness
- Rebound heatstroke within 48 hours
- Cardiac arrest; be ready to perform CPR

Frostnip – Ulcers Affecting the Extremities

Frostnip begins as firm, cold and white or gray areas on the face, ears, and extremities that can blister or peel just like sunburn as late as 2 to 3 days after the injury. The water in and around the cells freeze, rupturing cell walls, and damaging the tissue. Warming the affected area with hands or a warm object treats this injury. The positive side to an environment promoting frostnip is that zombies exposed to the same environment will become immobilized as temperatures drop towards freezing.

Trench Foot

Trench foot results from many hours or days of exposure to wet or damp conditions at a temperature just above freezing. In extreme cases the flesh dies and it may become necessary to have the foot or leg amputated. The best prevention is to keep your feet dry. Carry extra socks with you in a waterproof packet. Dry wet socks against your body. Wash your feet daily and put on dry socks. If your bug out location or temporary shelter promotes trench foot, someone in your group has made a seriously poor tactical decision. When you can, move locations.

Frostbite

This injury results from frozen tissues. Frostbite extends to a depth below the skin. The tissues become solid and immovable. Your feet, hands, and exposed facial areas are particularly vulnerable to frostbite.

Do not try to thaw the affected areas by placing them close to an open flame. Frostbitten tissue may be immersed in 99° to 109° F water until thawed. Dry the part and place it next to your skin to warm it at body temperature.

Hypothermia

Hypothermia is defined as the body's failure to maintain an inner core temperature of 97° F. Exposure to cool or cold temperature over time can cause hypothermia. Dehydration and lack of food and rest predispose the zombie survivalist to hypothermia.

Immediate treatment is the key. Move the victim to the best shelter possible away from the undead and elements. Remove all wet clothes and get the victim into dry clothing. Replace lost fluids with warm fluids, and warm them in a sleeping bag using two people (if possible) providing skin-to-skin contact. If the victim is unable to drink warm fluids, rectal rehydration may be used.

Diarrhea

Diarrhea is a common, debilitating ailment caused by changing water and food, drinking contaminated water, eating spoiled food, nervousness, becoming fatigued, and using dirty dishes. If you get diarrhea, limit your intake of fluids for 24 hours. Another solution is to drink one cup of a strong tea solution every 2 hours until the diarrhea slows or stops. The tannic acid in the tea helps to control the diarrhea. Boil the inner bark of a hardwood tree for 2 hours or more to release the tannic acid.

Intestinal Parasites

You can usually avoid worm infestations and other intestinal parasites if you take preventive measures. Never go barefoot. Avoid uncooked meat, never eat raw vegetables contaminated by raw sewage, and try not to use human waste as a fertilizer. Should you become infested and lack proper medicine, you can use:

- *Salt water.* Dissolve 4 tablespoons of salt in 1 liter of water and drink. Do not repeat this treatment.
- *Kerosene.* Drink 2 tablespoons of kerosene, **but no more**. If necessary, you can repeat this treatment in 24 to 48 hours. Be careful not to inhale the fumes.
- *Hot peppers.* Peppers are effective only if they are a steady part of your diet. You can eat them raw or put them in soups or rice and meat dishes.
- *Garlic.* Chop or crush 4 cloves, mix with 1 glass of liquid, and drink daily for 3 weeks.
- *Tobacco.* Eat 1 to 1 1/2 cigarettes or approximately 1 teaspoon (pinch) of smokeless tobacco. The nicotine in the tobacco will kill or stun the worms long enough for your system to pass them. If the infestation is severe, repeat the treatment in 24 to 48 hours, but no sooner.

NOTE: Tobacco and kerosene treatment techniques are very dangerous, be careful.

HERBAL MEDICINES

Our modern wonder drugs, laboratories, and equipment have obscured more primitive types of medicine involving determination, common sense, and a few simple treatments. However, the zombie apocalypse will return society, in many areas of the world, back to local "witch doctors" or healers to cure our ailments. Many of the herbs (plants) and treatments they use are as effective as the most modern medications available. In fact, many modern medications come from refined herbs.

> **WARNING**
> Use herbal medicines with extreme care, and only when you lack or have limited medical supplies. Some herbal medicines are dangerous and may cause further damage or even death.

In using plants for medical treatment, positive identification of the plants involved is as critical as when using them for food. Proper use of these plants is equally important.

Specific Remedies

The following remedies are for use only in a survival situation. Do not use them routinely as some can be potentially toxic and have serious long- term effects (for example, cancer).

- *Antidiarrheals for diarrhea.* This can be one of the most debilitating illnesses for a zombie survivalist. Drink tea made from the roots of blackberries to stop diarrhea. White oak bark and other barks containing tannin are also effective when made into a strong tea. However, because of possible negative effects on the kidneys, use them with caution and only when nothing else is available. Clay, ashes, charcoal, powdered chalk, powdered bones, and pectin can be consumed or mixed in a tannic acid tea with good results. These powdered mixtures should be taken in a dose of two tablespoons every 2 hours. Clay and pectin can be mixed together to give a crude form of Kaopectate. Pectin is obtainable from the inner part of citrus fruit rinds or from apple pomace. Because of its inherent danger to an already under-nourished survivor, several of these methods may need to be tried simultaneously to stop debilitating diarrhea, which can quickly dehydrate even a healthy individual.
- *Antiseptics to clean infections.* Use antiseptics to cleanse wounds, snake bites, sores, or rashes. You can make antiseptics from the juice of wild onion or garlic. Two of the best antiseptics are sugar and honey. Sugar should be applied to the wound until it becomes

syrupy, then washed off and reapplied. Honey should be applied three times daily. Honey is by far the best of the antiseptics for open wounds and burns.

- *Antipyretics for fevers.* Treat a fever with a tea made from willow bark.

- *Colds and sore throats.* Treat these illnesses with a tea made from willow bark.

- *Analgesics for aches, pains, and sprains.* Treat these conditions with externally applied mashed willow bark, or garlic. Chewing the willow bark or making a tea from it is the best for pain relief as it contains the raw component of aspirin. You can also use salves made by mixing the expressed juices of these plants in animal fat or vegetable oils.

- *Antihistamines and astringents for itching.* Relieve the itch from insect bites, sunburn, or plant poisoning rashes by applying aloe vera. In addition, dandelion sap, and crushed cloves of garlic have been used. Tobacco will deaden the nerve endings and can also be used to treat toothaches.

- *Hemorrhoids.* Treat them with external washes from elm or oak bark tea.

- *Heat rash.* Tannic acid will provide soothing relief because of its astringent properties but cornstarch or any crushed and powdered, nonpoisonous plant should help to dry out the rash after a thorough cleansing.

- *Constipation.* Relieve constipation by drinking tea from dandelion leaves, rose hips, or walnut bark. Eating raw daylily flowers will also help. Large amounts of water in any form are critical to relieving constipation.

- *Antifungal washes.* Make a tea of walnut leaves, oak bark, or acorns to treat ringworm and athlete's foot. Apply it frequently to the site, alternating with exposure to direct sunlight.

- *Burns.* Tannic acid, sugar, and honey can be used.

Tannic acid. Because tannic acid is used for so many treatments, a note as to its preparation is in order. All thready plants, especially trees, contain tannic acid. Hardwood trees generally contain more than softwood trees. Of the hardwoods, oak—especially red and chestnut—contain the highest amount. The warty looking knots in oak trees can contain as much as 28 percent tannic acid. This knot, the inner bark of trees, and pine needles (cut into 1-inch strips), can all be boiled down to extract tannic acid. Boiling can be done in as little as 15 minutes (very weak), to 2 hours (moderate), through 12 hours to 3 days (very strong). The stronger concoctions will have a dark color that will vary depending on the type of tree. All will have an increasingly vile taste in relation to their concentration.

Remember, any sign of the injured being infected, scratched, or bitten by the undead is a prompt to start handling them as the undead.

When the power grid fails, the water supplies in most cities will disappear almost overnight. Moments after the water pumps stop delivering to a city, supplies of bottled water will be stripped from the shelves.

The global zombie apocalypse will shut down most of the world's power grids for many months. No level of government will have the means to ensure every citizen gets the daily water they need to survive.

Because the typical person does not prepare for the zombie apocalypse, the crises will worsen as the unprepared become a burden to survivalists. Survivalists and groups that learn to procure water from sources other than the grid must rise and provide potable water to what is left of society.

6 - WATER PROCUREMENT

Water is one of your most urgent needs in a zombie survival situation. You cannot live long without it, especially in hot areas where you lose water rapidly through perspiration. Even in cold areas, you need a minimum of 2 liters of water each day to maintain efficiency.

More than three-fourths of your body is composed of fluids. Your body loses fluid because of heat, cold, stress, and exertion. To function effectively enough to survive the undead apocalypse, you must replace the fluid your body loses. One of your first goals is to obtain an adequate supply of water.

WATER SOURCES

Almost all environments have water, many with various sources.

NOTE: If you do not have a bottle, cup, can, or other type of container, improvise one from plastic or water-resistant cloth. Shape the plastic or cloth into a bowl by pleating it. Use pins or other suitable items—even your hands—to hold the pleats.

In **frigid climates**, good sources of water are snow and ice. To make it potable, melt and purify it. Do not ingest without first melting. Eating snow or ice can reduce body temperature and lead to more dehydration. Remember that snow and ice are no purer than the source water.

There are three sources of water when **at sea**. Water from the sea itself must be desalinated. Do not drink salted water. A second source of water, when at sea, is rain. Rain caught in tarps or other containers is salt free. If the tarp or other water-holding container is coated with salt, wash it in the sea before use to remove the majority of the salt. A third source of water when at sea is sea ice. Treat sea ice like any other ice from frigid areas, ensuring to desalt it as necessary.

In a **beach** environment, two water sources are ground and fresh. To collect ground water, dig a hole deep enough to allow water to seep into it. Drop fire-heated rocks into the water and collect the steam with an absorbent cloth. Wring the water from the cloth. If a pot is available, another approach is boiling the water and collecting the steam. Fresh water can be collected by digging behind the first group of sand dunes.

A **desert** environment creates the most challenging sources of water, so look:

- In deeply dug holes in valleys and low areas, at the foot of concave banks of dry rivers, at the foot of cliffs or rock outcrops, at the first depression behind the first sand dune of dry lakes, anywhere the surface sand is damp, and wherever you find green vegetation
- In pulp mashed from the top of cacti
- In depressions in holes in rocks, fissures in rocks, and porous rocks where it can be siphoned with a tube
- On metal, as condensation
- Along trails; watch for campsites and animal droppings indicating lines of traffic
- Where the birds congregate in the morning and evening

DO NOT substitute alcoholic beverages, urine, blood, or seawater for water. Alcoholic beverages dehydrate the body and cloud judgment, a fatal combination in areas of zombie infestation. Urine contains harmful bodily wastes and too high salt content. Blood is so salty it requires additional fluids to digest, and it can be a source of zombism. It takes twice the amount of salt free water to rid one's body of the damage by an amount of salty seawater. Please, do not drink your urine, and avoid the yellow snow.

Heavy dew can provide water. Tie rags or tufts of fine grass around your ankles and walk through dew-covered grass before sunrise. As the rags or grass tufts absorb the dew, wring the water into a container.

Bees or ants going into a hole in a tree may point to a water-filled hole. Water sometimes gathers in tree crotches or rock crevices. Siphon the water with plastic tubing or scoop it up with an improvised dipper. You can also stuff cloth in the hole to absorb the water and then wring it from the cloth.

Green bamboo thickets are an excellent source of fresh water. Water from green bamboo is clear and odorless. To get the water, bend a green bamboo stalk, tie it down, and cut off the top. The water will drip freely during the night. Old, cracked bamboo may also contain water. Purify this water before drinking.

Water From Green Bamboo

Some tropical vines can provide water. First, ensure the vine is not poisonous. Then, cut a notch in the vine as high as you can reach, then cut the vine off close to the ground. Catch the dropping liquid in a container or in your mouth.

The milk from young, green (unripe) coconuts is a good thirst quencher. However, the milk from mature, brown, coconuts contains oil that acts as a laxative. Drink in moderation only, and do not drink the liquid if it is sticky, milky, or bitter tasting. Laxatives and the aggressing undead are incompatible.

You can get water from plants with moist pulpy centers. Cut off a section of the plant and squeeze or smash the pulp so that the moisture runs out. Catch the liquid in a container.

Plant roots may provide water. Dig or pry the roots out of the ground, cut them into short pieces, and smash the pulp so that the moisture runs out. Catch the liquid in a container.

Fleshy leaves, stems, or stalks, such as bamboo, contain water. Cut or notch the stalks at the base of a joint to drain the liquid.

STILL CONSTRUCTION

If given enough time in a zombie free environment, you can use stills to draw moisture from the ground and from plant material. You need certain materials to build a still, and you need time to let it collect the water. It takes about 24 hours to get 0.5 to 1 liter of water.

Vegetation Bag Still

To make the vegetation bag still, you need a sunny slope on which to place the still, a clear plastic bag, green leafy vegetation, and a small rock.

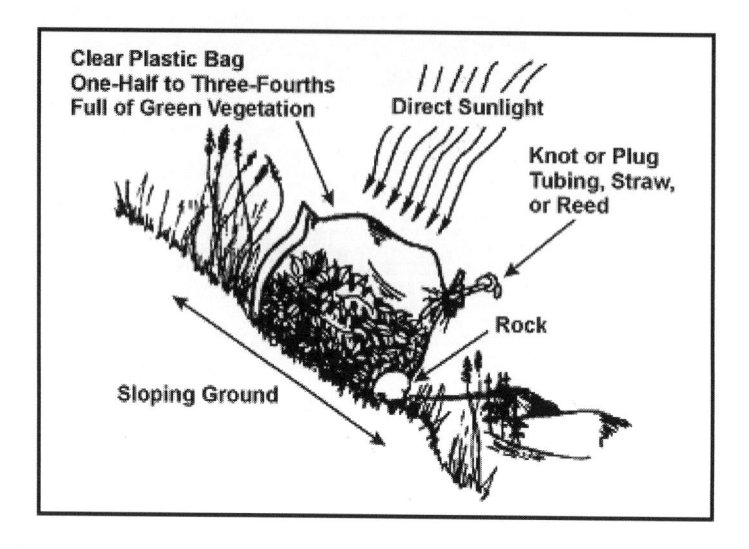

- Fill the plastic bag one-half to three-fourths full of green leafy vegetation. Be sure to remove all hard sticks or sharp spines that might puncture the bag. Be sure not to use poisonous vegetation.

- Place a small rock or similar item in the bag.

- Inflate the rest of the bag with air.

- Close the bag and tie the mouth securely as close to the end of the bag as possible to keep the maximum amount of air space. If you have a piece of tubing, a small straw, or a hollow reed, insert one end in the mouth of the bag before you tie it securely. Then tie off or plug the tubing so that air will not escape. This tubing will allow you to drain out condensed water without untying the bag.

- Place the bag, mouth downhill, on a slope in full sunlight. Position the mouth of the bag slightly higher than the low point in the bag.

- Settle the bag in place so that the rock works itself into the low point in the bag.

To get the condensed water from the still, loosen the tie around the bag's mouth and tip the bag so that the water collected around the rock will drain out. Retie the mouth securely and reposition the still to allow further condensation. Changing the vegetation in the bag after extracting most of the water from it will ensure maximum output of water.

Transpiration Bag Still

Making a transpiration bag still is similar to the vegetation bag, only easier. Ensuring the plant is not poisonous first, simply tie the plastic bag over a leafy tree limb with a tube inserted, and tie the mouth of the bag tightly around the branch to form an airtight seal. Tie the end of the limb so that it hangs below the level of the mouth of the bag. The water will collect there.

Water Transpiration Bag

Advantages to a transpiration bag still include:

- Only a plastic bag and rock are required
- Transpiration happens without manual intervention
- If done correctly, collected water is very clean

Belowground Still

To make a belowground still, you need a digging tool, a container, a clear plastic sheet, a drinking tube, and a rock.

Select a site where you believe the soil will contain moisture (such as a dry streambed or a low spot where rainwater has collected). The soil at this site should be easy to dig, and sunlight must hit the site most of the day.

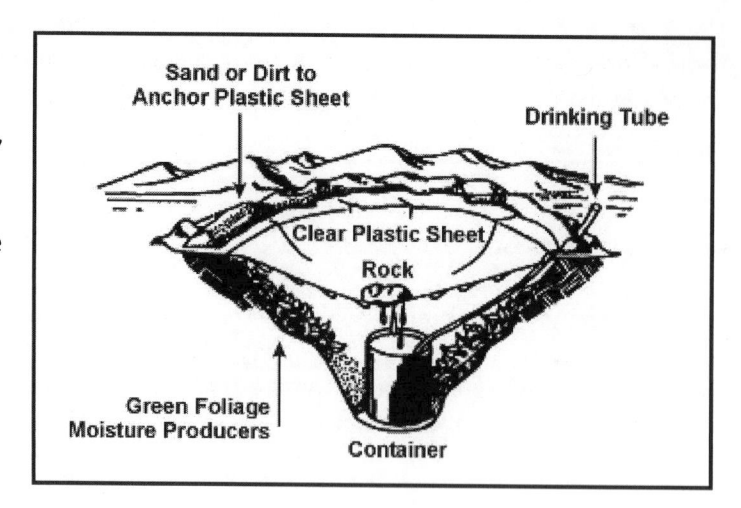

To construct the below ground still, you should—

- Dig a bowl-shaped hole about 3 feet across and 2 feet deep.
- Dig a sump in the center of the hole. The sump's depth and perimeter will depend on the size of the container you have to place in it.
- Anchor tubing to the container's bottom by forming a loose knot in the tubing.
- Place the container upright in the sump.
- Extend the unanchored end of the tubing up, over, and beyond the lip of the hole.
- Place the plastic sheet over the hole, covering its edges with soil to hold it in place.
- Place a rock in the center of the plastic sheet.
- Lower the plastic sheet into the hole until it is about 16 inches below ground level. It now forms an inverted cone with the rock at its apex. Make sure that the cone's apex is directly over your container. Also make sure the plastic cone does not touch the sides of the hole because the earth will absorb the condensed water.
- Put more soil on the plastic edges to secure its place and prevent moisture loss.
- Plug the tube when not in use to keep moisture from evaporating and to avoid insects.

Drink water without disturbing the still by using the tube as a straw. Opening the still undesirably releases the moist, warm air that has accumulated.

You may want to use plants in the hole as a moisture source. If so, dig additional soil from the sides of the hole to form a slope on which to place the plants. Then proceed as above.

You will need at least three stills to meet your individual daily water intake needs. In comparison to the belowground still and the water transpiration bag still, the vegetation bag produces the best yield of water.

WATER PURIFICATION

Rainwater collected in clean containers or in plants is usually safe for drinking. However, purify water from lakes, ponds, swamps, springs, or streams, especially the water near human settlements, downhill from farms or pastures, or in areas of high zombie infestation.

Prevalent pathogens found in water sources are commonly characterized by diarrhea, cramps, bloody stools, fever, weakness, vomiting, headache, jaundice, and parasites. By drinking nonpotable water you may contract diseases or swallow organisms that can harm you and may easily lead to potentially fatal waterborne illnesses, a fate as bad as contracting zombism.

When possible, purify all water you get from vegetation or from the ground by boiling or using water purification tablets. Boiling your drinking water is the safest method of purification. By achieving a rolling boil, you ensure that you are destroying all living waterborne pathogens.

While this is fair guidance for collecting water in a zombie survival situation, it should be complimented with field guides and hands-on training.

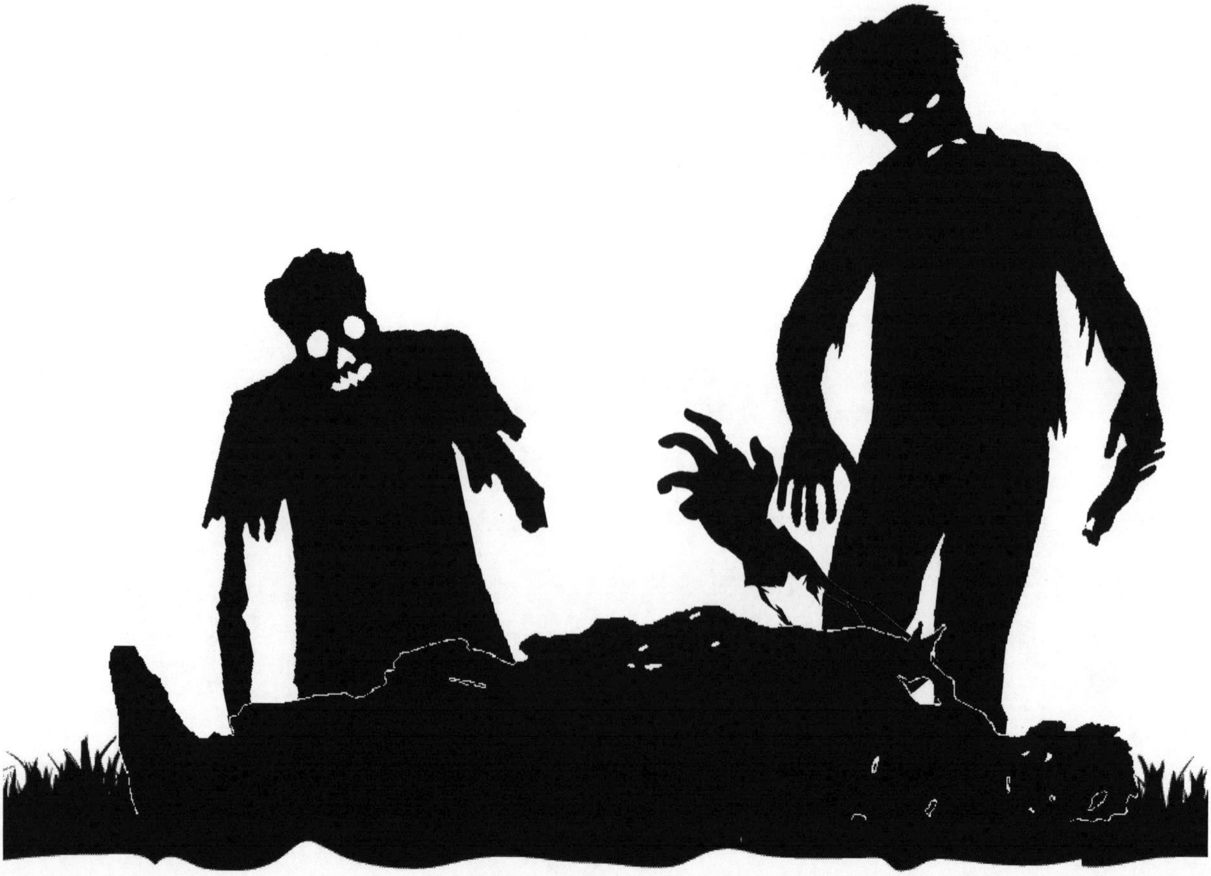

Every major city is within 3 days of the beginning of starvation. Once the widespread zombie outbreaks occur, panic and a failed transportation grid will close retail supply lines. A mad dash for the remaining resources will result in shelves empty of food.

But, food will remain abundant long after the supply trucks stop running and the farms and factories turn into hotspots of shotgun wielding survivors and undead campgrounds. We may have to adjust our perspective and put a little effort into procuring it, but we will be fine. Before grocery stores, and even before trading posts, humans lived off the land and its creatures with far less tools than we have today. Mammals, birds, fish, and vegetation will not only survive the zombie apocalypse, but will fare far better without so many of us living humans around. Take the time to learn to fish, hunt, identify edible plants, and build the confidence that you will live off these naturally unlimited sources of nutrition.

7 - FOOD PROCUREMENT

In addition to avoiding zombies, one of your most urgent requirements during the zombie apocalypse is food. In contemplating virtually any hypothetical zombie survival situation, the mind immediately turns to thoughts of food. Even water, which is more important to maintaining body functions, will usually follow food in our initial thoughts. The zombie survivalist must remember that the four essentials of survival—water, food, shelter, and avoiding the undead—are prioritized according to the situation. Prioritization must not only be timely, but accurate as well. We can live for weeks without food but it may take days or weeks to determine what is safe to eat and to trap animals in the area. Therefore, you need to begin food gathering in the earliest stages of surviving the zombie apocalypse as your endurance will decrease daily. Some situations may well dictate that defensive shelter precede both food and water.

Long Term Food

In preparation for the zombie apocalypse, part of your regular routine should include purchasing and storing long-term food. Long-term food includes items that can be stored up to 20 years. They are the foods with exceptionally long shelf life like powdered milk, dehydrated foods, and rice. Always rotate these foods using the FIFO system, First In, First Out, and store what you eat while you eat what you store, to further extend the shelf life. Keep a food stash at work, at home, and at your expected retreat location. Be prepared; do not starve.

Excellent choices for long term food include:

- Honey
- Peanut Butter
- Rice
- Dry Corn
- Wheat
- Oats / Oatmeal
- Beans
- Salt
- Macaroni
- Powdered Milk
- Potato Flakes
- Dried Fruits and Vegetables
- Sugar
- Canned Tuna
- Meals Ready to Eat (MRE)

Pet Food

If you have successfully stored an adequate supply of long shelf life food, when the shuffling dead arrive and the rest of society are caught in gun play as the grocery store shelves empty of food, consider heading to the local pet store. Reviewing the ingredients label on dog and cat foods may result in your identifying a more balanced diet than expected. Dog and cat foods may not be tasty, but they include many of the vitamins and minerals humans need to survive, and they last a very long time. Pet foods are generally low on Vitamin C, though, so plan ahead.

Vitamins

In a zombie survival situation, your food choices may quickly dwindle to less than a handful of sources. As such, multivitamins and supplements can increase your odds of staying healthy. While the benefits may not be required until after the first few months, multivitamins and supplements are lightweight and small enough to store and transport. Glucose tablets, in a zombie survival situation, can boost blood sugar levels for diabetics and provide boosts of energy.

ANIMALS FOR FOOD

Unless you have the chance to hunt large game, a real challenge when you yourself are being hunted by reanimated flesh eaters, concentrate your efforts on smaller animals. They are more abundant and easier to prepare.

You can, with relatively few exceptions, eat anything that crawls, swims, walks, or flies. You must first overcome your natural aversion to a particular food source. Historically, survivalists in zombie outbreaks have resorted to eating everything imaginable for nourishment. A person who ignores an otherwise healthy food source due to a personal bias, or because they feel it is unappetizing, is risking their own survival. Although it may prove difficult at first, you must eat what is available to maintain your health. Some classes of animals and insects may be eaten raw if necessary, but you should, if possible, thoroughly cook all food sources whenever possible to avoid illness.

Insects

The most abundant and easily caught life-form on Earth are insects. Many insects provide 65 to 80 percent protein compared to beef's 20 percent. This makes insects an important, if not appetizing, food source. Insects to avoid include all adults that sting or bite, hairy or brightly colored insects, and caterpillars and insects that have a pungent odor. Avoid spiders and common disease carriers such as ticks, flies, and mosquitoes.

After ensuring the area is free of zombies, rotting logs lying on the ground are excellent places to look for a variety of insects including ants, termites, beetles, and grubs, which are beetle larvae. Grassy areas, such as fields, are good areas to search because the insects are easily seen, but zombies can see you better in large open spaces, so beware of local zombie activity. Stones, boards, or other materials lying on the ground provide the insects with good nesting sites. Insect larvae are also edible. Insects that have a hard outer shell such as beetles and grasshoppers will have parasites. Cook them before eating. Remove any wings and barbed legs also. You can eat most soft-shelled insects raw. The taste varies from one species to another. Wood grubs are bland, but some species of ants store honey in their bodies, giving them a sweet taste. You can grind a collection of insects into a paste, mix them with edible vegetation, or cook them to improve their taste.

Worms

Worms are an excellent protein source. Dig for them in damp soil and grass clumps, or watch for them on the ground after a rain. Put them in clean, potable water for 15 minutes. The worms will naturally purge or wash themselves out, after which they can be eaten raw.

Crustaceans

Freshwater shrimp can form rather large colonies in mats of floating algae or in mud bottoms of ponds and lakes. Do not forget that zombies can live under water and in mud, so be aware!

There are two easy ways to catch crayfish. You can catch crayfish by tying bits of internal organs to a string. When the crayfish grabs the bait, pull it to shore before it has a chance to release the bait. Or, you can place a bucket behind the crayfish and use a tickle stick to coax it into retreating into the bucket.

You can find saltwater lobsters, crabs, and shrimp from the surf's edge out to water 30 feet deep. Shrimp may come to a light at night where you can scoop them up with a net. You can catch lobsters and crabs with a baited trap or a baited hook. Crabs will come to bait placed at the edge of the surf, where you can trap or net them. Lobsters and crabs are nocturnal and caught best at night. Remember, zombies do not need light for direction, so always practice good zombie avoidance at night.

NOTE: You must cook all freshwater crustaceans, mollusks, and fish. As if the shuffling horrors are not enough to worry about, fresh water tends to harbor many dangerous organisms, animal and human contaminants, and pollutants.

Mollusks

Mollusks include octopuses and freshwater and saltwater shellfish such as snails, clams, mussels, bivalves, barnacles, periwinkles, chitons, and sea urchins. Bivalves similar to freshwater mussel and terrestrial and aquatic snails live worldwide under all water conditions.

In fresh water, avoiding the submerged undead, look for mollusks in the shallows, especially in water with a sandy or muddy bottom.

Near the sea, look in the tidal pools and the wet sand. Rocks along beaches or extending as reefs into deeper water often bear clinging shellfish. Snails and limpets cling to rocks and seaweed from the low water mark upward. Large snails, called chitons, adhere tightly to rocks above the surf line.

Mussels usually form dense colonies in rock pools, on logs, or at the base of boulders.

Caution: If a noticeable red tide has occurred within 72 hours, do not eat any fish or shellfish from that water source. Do not eat shellfish that are not covered by water at high tide!

Fish

Fish represent a good source of protein and fat. They offer distinct advantages to the zombie apocalypse survivor. They are usually more abundant than mammal wildlife, and the ways to get them are silent – which is much preferred when avoiding the shuffling horrors. To be successful at catching fish, you must know their habits. For instance, fish tend to feed heavily before a storm. Fish are not likely to feed after a storm when the water is muddy and swollen. Light often attracts fish (but also zombies) at night. When there is a heavy current, fish will rest in places where there is an eddy, such as near rocks. Fish will also gather where there are deep pools, under overhanging brush, and in and around submerged foliage, logs, or other objects that offer them shelter. Unfortunately, zombies are also known to be found in the same areas.

There are no naturally poisonous freshwater fish, but cook all freshwater fish to kill parasites. As a precaution, also cook saltwater fish caught within a reef or within the influence of a freshwater source. Any marine life obtained farther out in the sea will not contain parasites because of the saltwater environment. You can eat these raw.

Most fish encountered are edible. The organs of some species are always poisonous to man; other fish can become toxic because of elements in their diets. Ciguatera is a form of human poisoning, almost as bad as zombism, caused by the consumption of subtropical and tropical marine fish which have accumulated naturally occurring toxins through their diet. Marine fish most commonly implicated in ciguatera poisoning include the barracudas, jacks, mackerel, triggerfish, snappers, and groupers. Anyone who has had food poisoning can tell you that it would be tough to deal with it and the zombie outbreak at the same time. Other examples of poisonous saltwater fish are the porcupine fish, cowfish, thorn fish, oilfish, and puffer.

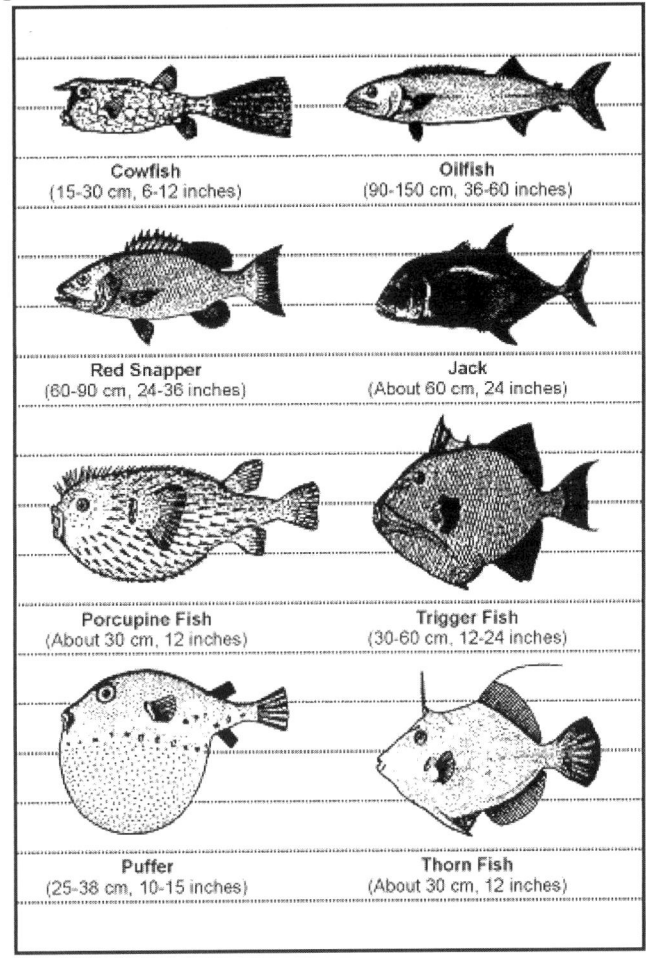

Cowfish (15-30 cm, 6-12 inches)	Oilfish (90-150 cm, 36-60 inches)
Red Snapper (60-90 cm, 24-36 inches)	Jack (About 60 cm, 24 inches)
Porcupine Fish (About 30 cm, 12 inches)	Trigger Fish (30-60 cm, 12-24 inches)
Puffer (25-38 cm, 10-15 inches)	Thorn Fish (About 30 cm, 12 inches)

Amphibians

Frogs are easily found around bodies of fresh water, near the safety of the water's edge. At the first sign of danger, they plunge into the water and bury themselves with trapped zombies in the mud and debris. Frogs are characterized by smooth, moist skin. The few poisonous species of frogs include any brightly colored frog or one that has a distinct "X" mark on its back as well as all tree frogs. Do not confuse toads with frogs. Toads may be recognized by their dry, "warty" or bumpy skin. They are usually found on land in drier environments. Several species of toads secrete a poisonous substance through their skin as a defense against attack. Therefore, to avoid poisoning, do not handle or eat toads.

Do not eat salamanders; only about 25 percent of all salamanders are edible, so it is not worth the risk of selecting a poisonous variety. Salamanders are found around the water. They are characterized by smooth, moist skin and have only four toes on each foot.

Reptiles

Reptiles are a good protein source and relatively easy to catch. Thorough cooking and hand washing is imperative with reptiles. All reptiles are considered to be carriers of salmonella, which exists naturally on their skin. Turtles and snakes are especially known to infect humans. If you are in an undernourished state and your immune system is weak, salmonella can be as deadly as a zombie bite. Cook food thoroughly and scrupulously wash your hands after handling any reptile. Lizards are plentiful in most parts of the world. They may be recognized by their dry, scaly skin. They have five toes on each foot. The only poisonous ones are the Gila monster and the Mexican beaded lizard. Care must be taken when handling and preparing the iguana and the monitor lizard, as they commonly harbor the salmonella virus in their mouth and teeth. The tail meat is the best tasting and easiest to prepare.

Turtles are a very good source of meat. Most of the meat will come from the front and rear shoulder area, although a large turtle may have some on its neck. The box turtle is a commonly encountered turtle that you SHOULD NOT eat. It feeds on poisonous mushrooms and may build up a highly toxic poison in its flesh. Also avoid the hawksbill turtle, found in the Atlantic Ocean, because of its poisonous thorax gland. Poisonous snakes, alligators, crocodiles, and large sea turtles present obvious hazards to the zombie survivalist.

Birds

All species of birds are edible. The only poisonous bird is the Pitohui, native only to New Guinea. You may skin fish-eating birds to improve their taste. As with any wild animal, you must understand birds' common habits to have a realistic chance of capturing them. You can take pigeons, as well as some other species, from their roost at night by hand. During the nesting season, some species will not leave the nest even when approached. Knowing where and when the birds nest makes catching them easier. Birds tend to have regular flyways going from the roost to a feeding area, to water, and so forth. Careful observation should reveal where these flyways are and indicate good areas for catching birds in nets stretched across the flyways. Roosting sites and waterholes are some of the most promising areas for trapping or snaring.

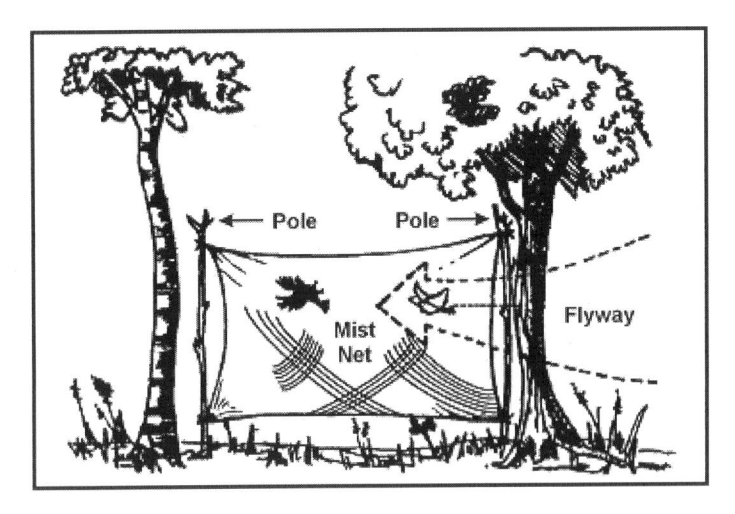

Nesting birds present another food source—eggs. Remove all but two or three eggs from the clutch, marking the ones that you leave. The bird will continue to lay more eggs to fill the clutch. Continue removing the fresh eggs, leaving the ones you marked.

Mammals

Mammals are excellent protein sources and have the most nutrition pound per pound. There are some drawbacks to obtaining mammals. In a zombie-infested environment, the undead may be caught in traps or snares meant for animals. The amount of injury an animal can inflict is in direct proportion to its size. All mammals have teeth and nearly all will bite in self-defense. Even a squirrel can inflict a serious wound and any bite presents a risk of infection. Also, any mother can be extremely aggressive in defense of her young. Any animal with no route of escape will fight when cornered.

All mammals are edible; however, the polar bear and bearded seal have toxic levels of vitamin A in their livers. The platypus, native to Australia and Tasmania, is an egg-laying, semiaquatic mammal that has poisonous claws on its hind legs. Scavenging mammals, such as the opossum, may carry diseases.

TRAPS AND SNARES

For an unarmed zombie apocalypse survivor, or when the sound of a rifle shot could attract the undead, trapping or snaring wild game is a good alternative. Several well-placed traps have the potential to catch much more game than a person with a rifle is likely to shoot. To be effective with any type of trap or snare, you must—

- Be familiar with the species of animal you intend to catch.
- Be capable of constructing a proper trap and properly masking your scent.
- Not alarm the prey by leaving signs of your presence.

There are no catchall traps you can set for all animals. You must determine what species are in the area and set your traps specifically with those animals in mind. Look for the following:

- Runs and trails
- Tracks
- Droppings
- Chewed or rubbed vegetation
- Nesting or roosting sites
- Feeding and watering areas

Position your traps and snares where there is proof that animals pass through, but little signs of zombie activity. You must determine if it is a "run" or a "trail." A trail will show signs of use by several species and will be rather distinct. A run is usually smaller and less distinct and will only contain signs of one species. You may construct a perfect snare, but it will not catch anything if haphazardly placed in the woods. Animals have bedding areas, water holes, and feeding areas with trails leading from one to another. You must place snares and traps around these areas to be effective.

If you are in an active zombie environment, out of the way trap and snare placement is important. However, it is equally important not to create a disturbance that will alarm the animal and cause it to avoid the trap. Therefore, if you must dig, remove all fresh dirt from the area. Most animals will instinctively avoid a pitfall-type trap. Prepare the various parts of a trap or snare away from the site, carry them in, and set them up. Such actions make it easier to avoid disturbing the local vegetation, thereby alerting the prey. Do not use freshly cut, live vegetation to construct a trap or snare. Freshly cut vegetation will "bleed" sap that has an odor the prey will be able to smell. It is an alarm signal to the animal.

You must remove or mask the human scent on and around the trap you set. Although birds do not have a developed sense of smell, nearly all mammals depend on smell even more than on sight. Even the slightest human scent on a trap will alarm the prey and cause it to avoid the area. Actually removing the scent from a trap is difficult but masking it is relatively easy. Use the fluid from the gall and urine bladders of previous kills. Do not use human urine. Mud, particularly from an area with plenty of rotting vegetation, is also good. Use it to coat your hands when handling the trap and to coat the trap when setting it. In nearly all parts of the world, animals know the smell of burned vegetation and smoke. It is only when a fire is actually burning that they become alarmed. Therefore, smoking the trap parts is an effective means to mask your scent. If one of the above techniques is not practical, and if time permits, allow a trap to weather for a few days and then set it. Do not handle a trap while it is weathering. Position traps away from zombie activity to prevent accidental destruction by the stumbling undead, and to avoid alarming the prey.

Traps or snares placed on a trail or run should use funneling or channelization. To build a channel, construct a funnel-shaped barrier extending from the sides of the trail toward the trap, with the narrowest part nearest the trap. Channelization should be inconspicuous to avoid alerting the prey. As the animal gets to the trap, it cannot turn left or right and continues into the trap. Few wild animals will back up, preferring to face the direction of travel. Channelization does not have to be an impassable barrier. You only have to make it inconvenient for the animal to go over or through the barrier. For best effect, the channelization should reduce the trail's width to just slightly wider than the targeted animal's body. Maintain this constriction at least as far back from the trap as the animal's body length, then begin the widening toward the mouth of the funnel.

Bait

Baiting a trap or snare increases your chances of catching an animal. When catching fish, you must bait nearly all devices. Success with an unbaited trap depends on its placement in a good location. A baited trap can actually draw animals to it. The bait should be something the animal knows. However, this bait should not be so readily available in the immediate area that the animal can get it close by. For example, baiting a trap with corn in the middle of a cornfield would not be likely to work. Likewise, if corn is not grown in the region, a corn-baited trap may arouse an animal's curiosity and keep it alerted while it ponders the strange food. Under such circumstances it may not go for the bait. One bait that works well on small mammals is peanut butter. Scatter bits of bait around the trap to give the prey a chance to sample it and develop a craving for it. The animal will then overcome some of its caution before it gets to the trap.

If you set and bait a trap for one species but another species takes the bait without being caught, try to determine what the animal was. Then set a proper trap for that animal, using the same bait.

Once you have successfully trapped an animal, you will not only gain confidence in your ability, you will also have resupplied yourself with bait for several more traps. Start practicing now.

Construction

Traps and snares crush, choke, hang, or entangle prey. As such, they are proven to attract the flesh eaters. Always be aware of the undead in areas of animal commotion. A single trap or snare will commonly incorporate two or more of these principles.

The heart of any trap or snare is the trigger. When planning a trap or snare, ask yourself how it should affect the prey, what is the source of power, and what will be the most efficient trigger. Your answers will help you devise a specific trap for a specific species. Traps are designed to catch and hold or to catch and kill. Snares are traps that incorporate a noose to accomplish either function.

Simple Snare

A simple snare consists of a noose placed over a trail or den hole and attached to a firmly planted stake. If the noose is some type of cordage placed upright on a game trail, use small twigs or blades of grass to hold it up. Make sure the noose is large enough to pass freely over the animal's head. As the animal continues to move, the noose tightens around its neck. The more the animal struggles, the tighter the noose gets. This type of snare usually does not kill the animal. Wire is the best choice for a simple snare.

Try your best not to snare a zombie. It is such a bad idea, I do not know where to start.

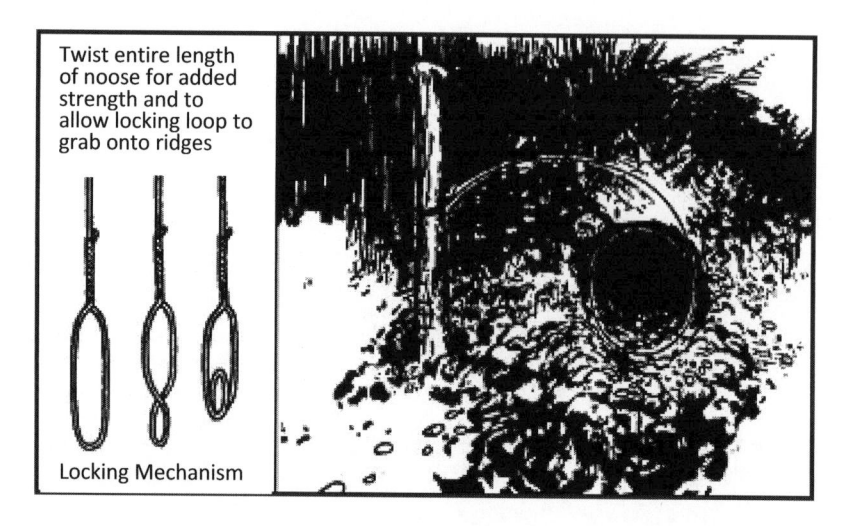

Simple Snare

Drag Noose

Use a drag noose on an animal run. Place forked sticks on either side of the run and lay a sturdy crossmember across them. Tie the noose to the crossmember and hang it at a height above the animal's head. (Nooses designed to catch by the head should never be low enough for the prey to step into with a foot.) As the noose tightens around the animal's neck, the animal pulls the crossmember from the forked sticks and drags it. The surrounding vegetation quickly catches the crossmember and the animal becomes entangled.

Try your best not to drag noose a zombie. Again, it is such a bad idea.

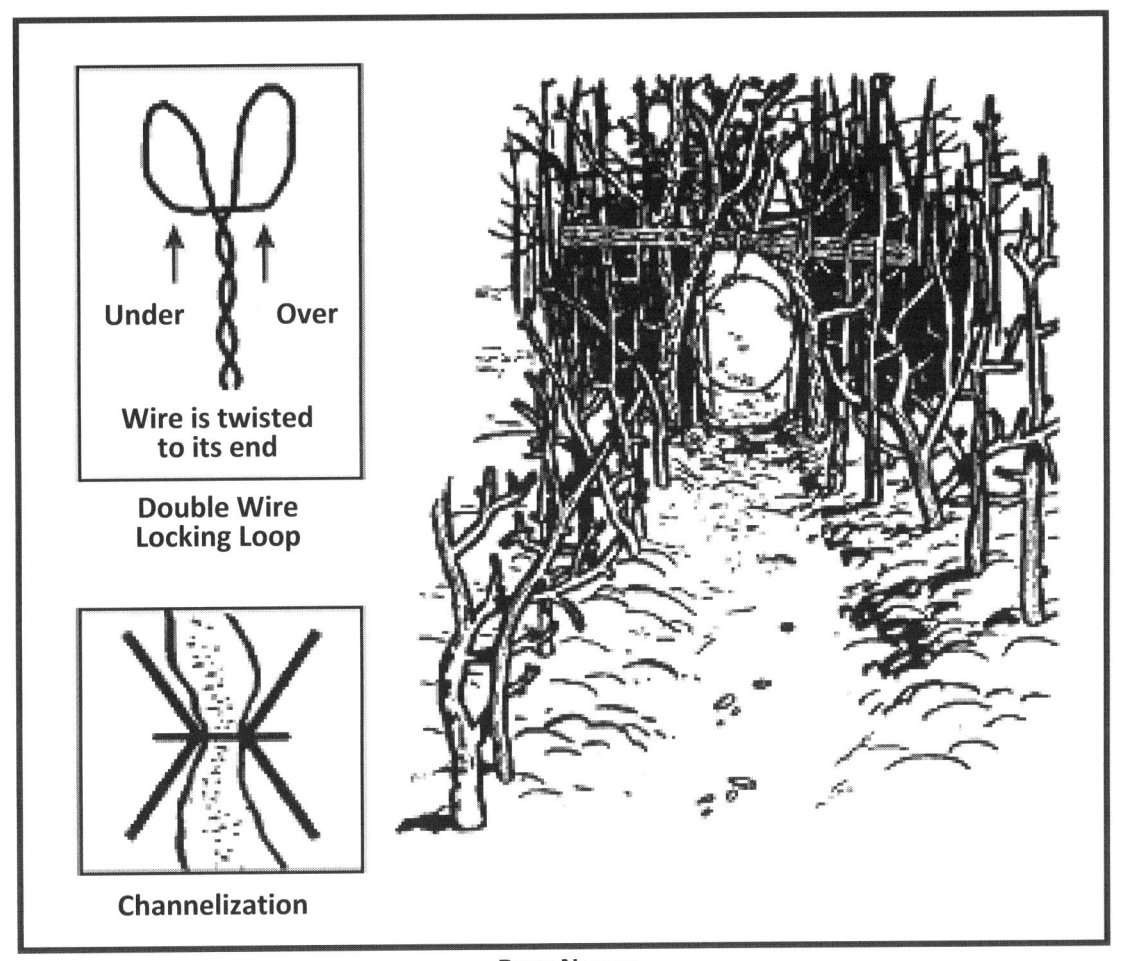

Drag Noose

Twitch-Up

A twitch-up is a supple sapling that, when bent over and secured with a triggering device, will provide power to a variety of snares. Select a hickory or other hardwood sapling along the trail. A twitch-up will work much faster and with more force if you remove all the branches and foliage.

Twitch-Up Snare

A simple twitch-up snare uses two forked sticks, each with a long and short leg. Bend the twitch-up and mark the trail below it. Drive the long leg of one forked stick firmly into the ground at that point. Ensure the cut on the short leg of this stick is parallel to the ground. Tie the long leg of the remaining forked stick to a piece of cordage secured to the twitch-up. Cut the short leg so that it catches on the short leg of the other forked stick. Extend a noose over the trail. Set the trap by bending the twitch-up and engaging the short legs of the forked sticks. When an animal catches its head in the noose, it pulls the forked sticks apart, allowing the twitch-up to spring up and hang the prey.

NOTE: Do not use green sticks for the trigger. The sap that oozes out could glue them together.

Twitch-Up Snare

Squirrel Pole

A squirrel pole is a long pole placed against a tree in an area of frequent squirrel activity. Place several wire nooses along the top and sides of the pole so that a squirrel trying to go up or down the pole will have to pass through one or more of them. Position the nooses (2 to 2 1/4-inches in diameter) about 1 inch off the pole. Place the top and bottom wire nooses 18 inches from the top and bottom of the pole to prevent the squirrel from getting its feet on a solid surface. If this happens, the squirrel will chew through the wire. Squirrels are naturally curious. After an initial period of caution, they will try to go up or down the pole and will be caught in the noose. The struggling animal will soon fall from the pole and strangle. Other squirrels will soon be drawn to the commotion. In this way, you can catch several squirrels. You can emplace multiple poles to increase the catch.

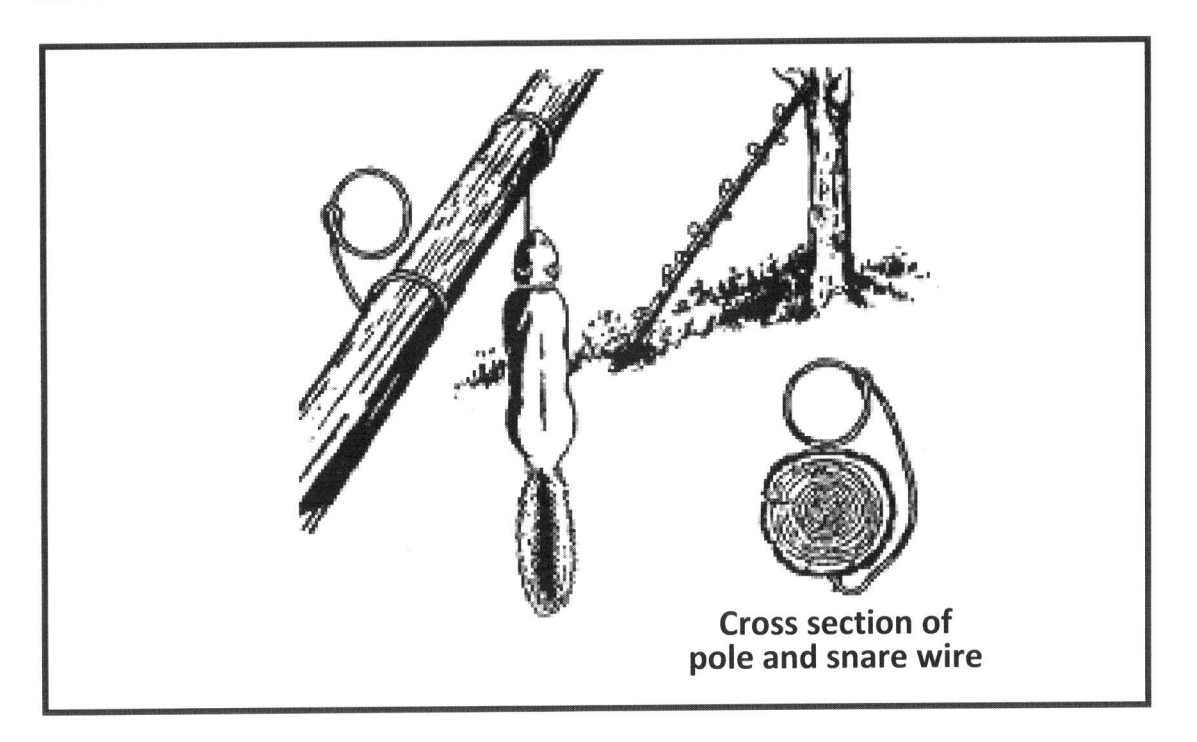

Squirrel Pole

Noosing Wand

A noose stick or "noosing wand" is useful for capturing roosting birds or small mammals. It requires a patient operator in a zombie free area. This wand is more a weapon than a trap. It consists of a pole (as long as you can effectively handle) with a slip noose of wire or stiff cordage at the small end. To catch an animal, you slip the noose over the neck of a roosting bird and pull it tight. You can also place it over a den hole and hide in a nearby blind. When the animal emerges from the den, you jerk the pole to tighten the noose and thus capture the animal. Carry a stout club to kill the prey. This is not an efficient tool for the undead.

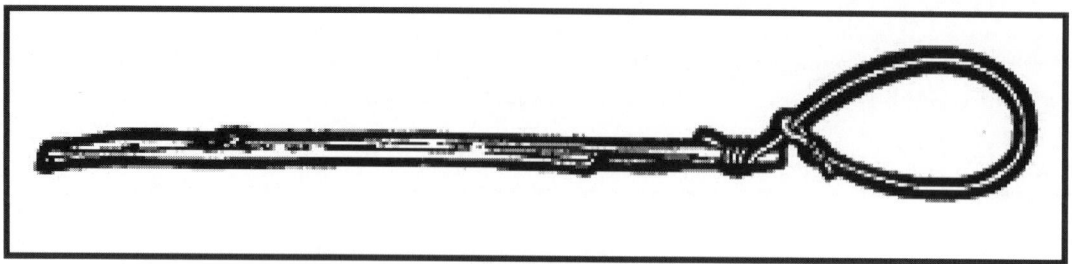

Noosing Wand

Figure 4 Deadfall

The figure 4 deadfall is a trigger used to drop a weight onto a prey and crush it. The type of weight used may vary, but it should be heavy enough to kill or incapacitate the prey immediately. Construct the figure 4 using three notched sticks. These notches hold the sticks together in a figure 4 pattern when under tension. Practice making this trigger beforehand; it requires close tolerances and precise angles in its construction.

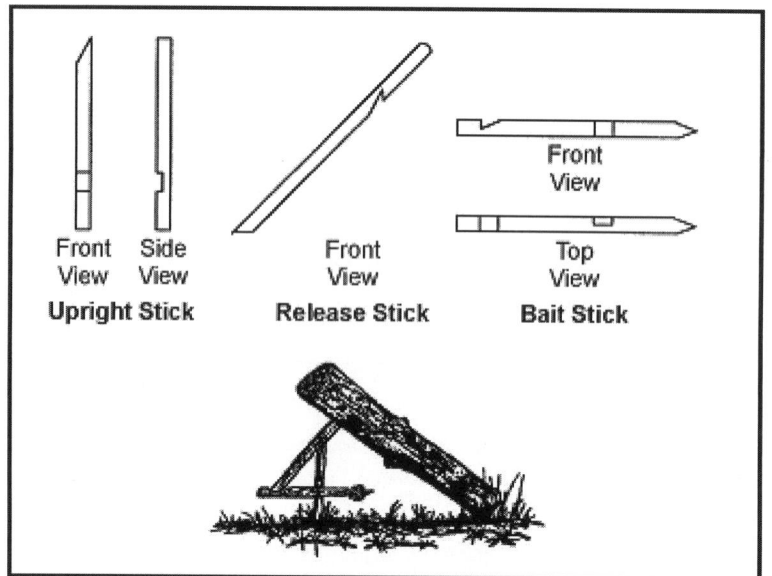

Figure 4 Deadfall

Bottle Trap

A bottle trap is a simple trap for mice and voles. Dig a hole 12 to 18 inches deep that is wider at the bottom than at the top. Make the top of the hole as small as possible. Place a piece of bark or wood over the hole with small stones under it to hold it up 1 to 2 inches off the ground. Mice or voles will hide under the cover to escape danger and fall into the hole. They cannot climb out because of the wall's backward slope. Use caution when checking this trap; it is an excellent hiding place for snakes.

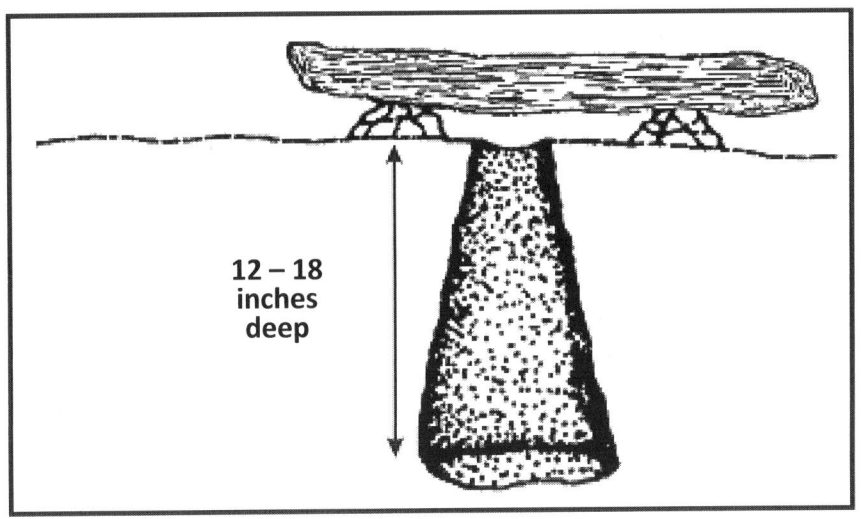

Bottle Trap

KILLING DEVICES

The rabbit stick, and the spear are killing devices that you can construct to help you obtain small game to help you survive.

Rabbit Stick

One of the simplest and most effective killing devices is a stout stick as long as your arm, from fingertip to shoulder, called a "rabbit stick." You can throw it either overhand or sidearm and with considerable force. It is best thrown so that it flies sideways, increasing the chance of hitting the target. It is very effective against small game that stops and freezes as a defense.

Spear

You can make a spear to kill small game and to fish, but not the undead. Jab with the spear—do not throw it. An explanation of spearfishing follows.

FISHING DEVICES

You can make your own fishhooks, nets, and traps. The paragraphs below discuss several methods to obtain fish.

Improvised Fishhooks

You can make practical fishhooks from pins, needles, wire, small nails, or any piece of metal. You can also use wood, bone, coconut shell, thorns, flint, seashell, or tortoise shell. You can also make fishhooks from any combination of these items.

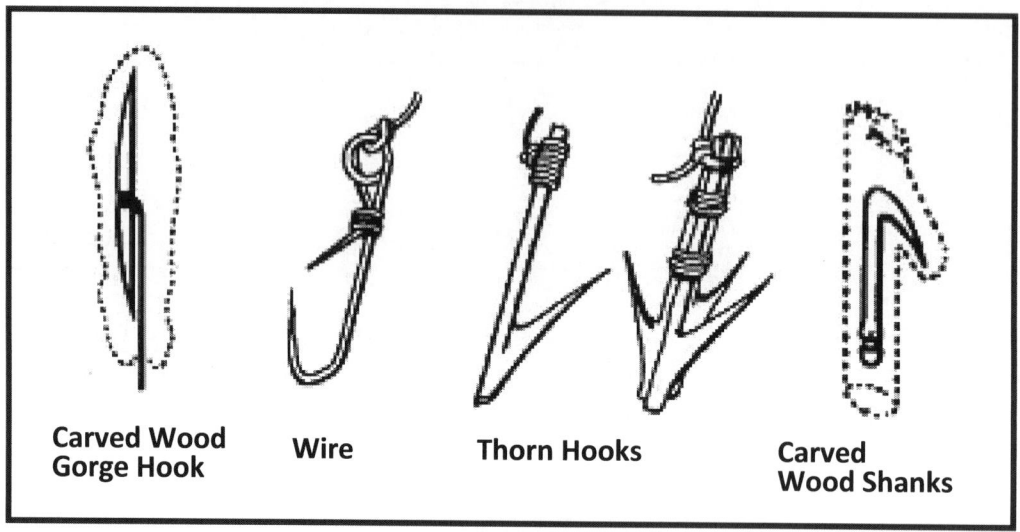

Carved Wood Gorge Hook   **Wire**   **Thorn Hooks**   **Carved Wood Shanks**

Improvised Fishhooks

To make a wooden hook, cut a piece of hardwood about 1 inch long and about 1/4 inch in diameter to form the shank. Cut a notch in one end in which to place the point. Place the point (piece of bone, wire, nail) in the notch. Hold the point in the notch and tie securely so that it does not move out of position. This is a fairly large hook. To make smaller hooks, use smaller material.

A gorge or skewer is a small shaft of wood, bone, metal, or other material. It is sharp on both ends and notched in the middle where you tie cordage. Bait the gorge by placing a piece of bait on it lengthwise. When the fish swallows the bait, it also swallows the gorge. If you are tending the fishing line when the fish bites, do not attempt to pull on the line to set the hook as you would with a conventional hook. Allow the fish to swallow the bait to get the gorge as far down its throat before the gorge sets itself.

Stakeout

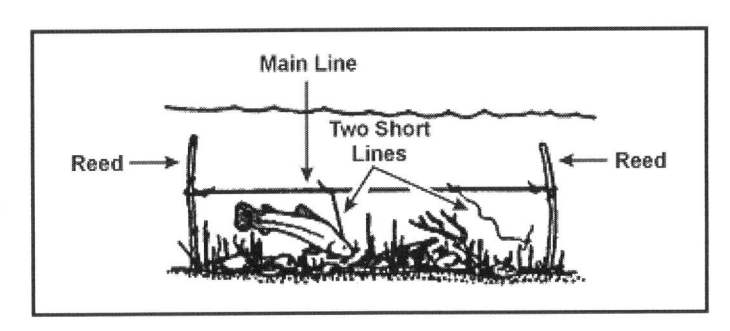

A stakeout is a fishing device you can use in an active zombie environment. To construct a stakeout, drive two supple saplings into the bottom of the lake, pond, or stream with their tops just below the water surface. Tie a cord between them just slightly below the surface. Tie two short cords with hooks or gorges to this cord, ensuring that they cannot wrap around the poles or each other. They should also not slip along the long cord. Bait the hooks or gorges.

Spearfishing

If you are near shallow water (about waist deep) where the fish are large and plentiful, you can spear them. To make a spear, cut a long, straight sapling. Sharpen the end to a point or attach a knife, jagged piece of bone, or sharpened metal. You can also make a spear by splitting the shaft a few inches down from the end and inserting a piece of wood to act as a spreader. You then sharpen the two separated halves to points. To spear fish, find an area where fish either gather or where there is a fish run. Place the spear point into the water and slowly move it toward the fish. Then, with a sudden push, impale the fish on the stream bottom. Do not try to lift the fish with the spear, as it will probably slip off and you will lose it; hold the spear with one hand and grab and hold the fish with the other. Do not throw the spear, especially if the point is a knife. You cannot afford to lose a knife in a zombie survival situation. Be alert to the problems caused by light refraction when looking at objects in the water. You must aim lower than the object, usually at the bottom of the fish, to hit your mark.

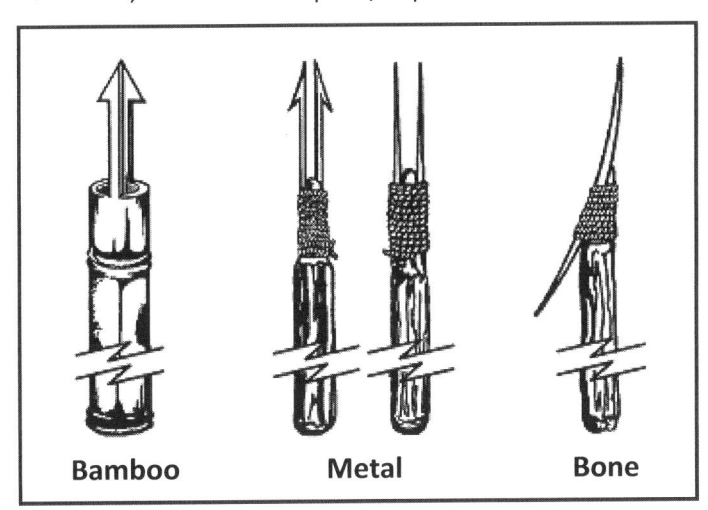

Types of Spear Points

COOKING AND STORAGE OF FISH AND GAME

You must know how to prepare fish and game for cooking and storage in a zombie survival situation. Improper cleaning or storage can result in inedible fish or game.

Fish

Do not eat fish that appears spoiled. Cooking does not ensure that spoiled fish will be edible. Signs of spoilage are—

- Sunken eyes
- Peculiar odor
- Suspicious color (Gills should be red to pink. Scales should be a pronounced shade of gray, not faded.)
- Dents that stay in the fish's flesh after pressed with your thumb
- Slimy, rather than moist or wet, body
- Sharp or peppery taste

Eating spoiled or rotten fish may cause diarrhea, nausea, cramps, vomiting, itching, paralysis, or a metallic taste in the mouth. Induce vomiting if symptoms appear. These symptoms are undesirable while trying to avoid advancing hordes of soulless human corpses.

Fish spoils quickly after death, especially on a hot day. Prepare fish for eating as soon as possible after catching it. Cut out the gills and the large blood vessels that lie near the spine. Gut fish that are more than 4 inches long. Scale or skin the fish.

You can impale a whole fish on a stick and cook it over an open fire. However, boiling the fish with the skin on is the best way to get the most food value. The fats and oil are under the skin and, by boiling, you can save the juices for broth. Pack fish into a ball of clay and bury it in the coals of a fire until the clay hardens. Break open the clay ball to get to the cooked fish. Fish is done when the meat flakes off. If you plan to keep the fish for later, smoke or fry it. To prepare fish for smoking, cut off the head and remove the backbone.

Snakes

To skin a snake, first cut off its head, to include 4 to 6 inches behind the head. This will ensure you remove the venom sac, which is located at the base of the head. Then cut the skin down the body 1 to 1 1/2 inches. Peel the skin back, then grasp the skin in one hand and the body in the other and pull apart. On large, bulky snakes it may be necessary to slit the belly skin. Cook snakes in the same manner as small game. Remove the entrails and discard. Cut the snake into small sections and boil or roast it.

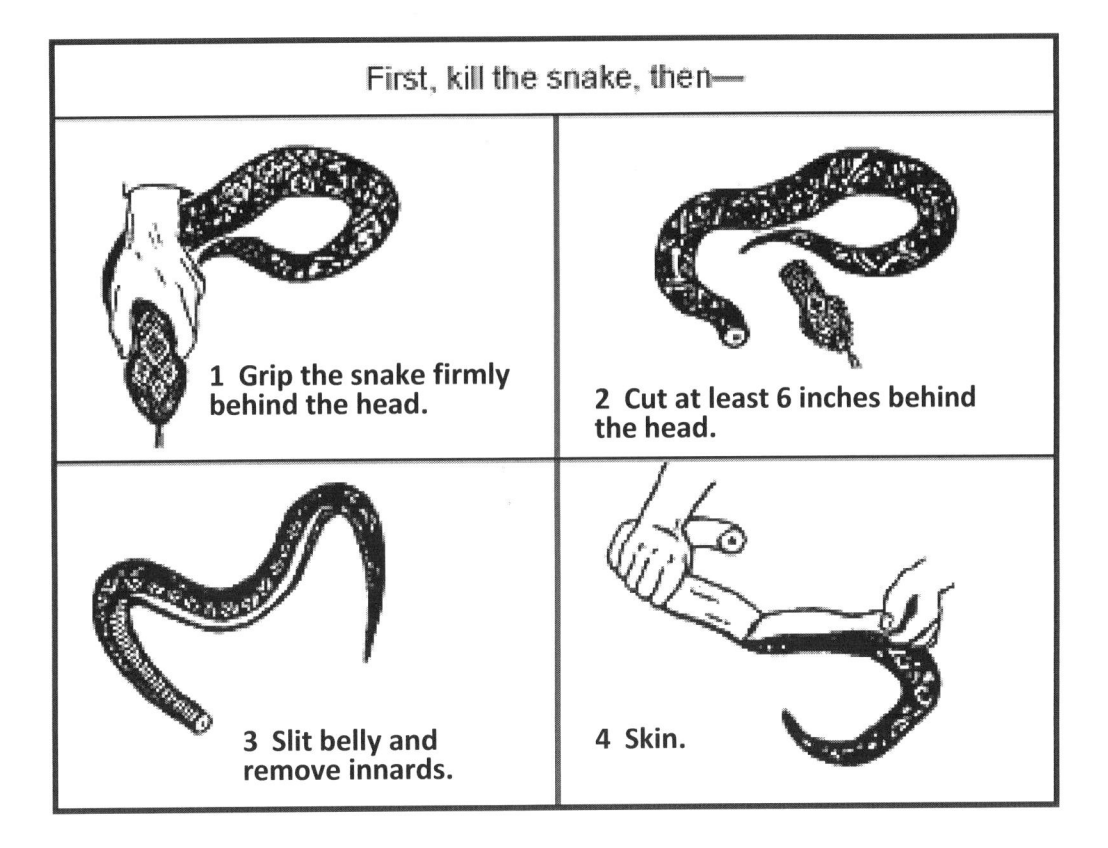

First, kill the snake, then—

1 Grip the snake firmly behind the head.

2 Cut at least 6 inches behind the head.

3 Slit belly and remove innards.

4 Skin.

Birds

After killing the bird, remove its feathers by either plucking or skinning. Remember, skinning removes some of the food value. Open the body cavity and remove the entrails, heart, and liver. Cut off the feet. Cook by boiling or roasting over a spit. Before cooking scavenger birds, boil them at least 20 minutes to kill parasites.

Skinning and Butchering Game

Ensuring a zombie free area, bleed the animal by cutting its throat. If possible, clean the carcass near a stream. Place the carcass belly up and split the hide from throat to tail, cutting around all sexual organs. Remove the musk glands at points A and B to avoid tainting the meat. For smaller mammals, cut the hide around the body and insert two fingers under the hide on both sides of the cut and pull off both pieces.

NOTE: When cutting the hide, insert the knife blade under the skin and turn the blade up so that only the hide gets cut. This will also prevent cutting hair and getting it on the meat.

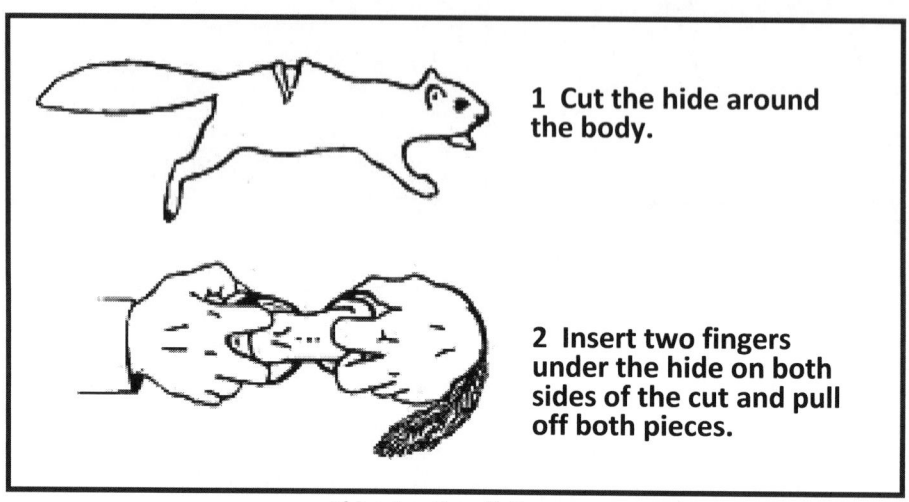

1 Cut the hide around the body.

2 Insert two fingers under the hide on both sides of the cut and pull off both pieces.

Skinning Small Game

Remove the entrails from smaller game by splitting the body open and pulling them out with the fingers. Do not forget the chest cavity. For larger game, cut the gullet away from the diaphragm. Roll the entrails out of the body. Cut around the anus, then reach into the lower abdominal cavity, grasp the lower intestine, and pull to remove. Remove the urine bladder by pinching it off and cutting it below the fingers. If you spill urine on the meat, wash it to avoid tainting the meat. Save the heart and liver. Cut these open and inspect for signs of worms or other parasites. Also inspect the liver's color; it could indicate a diseased animal. The liver's surface should be smooth and wet and its color deep red or purple. If the liver appears diseased, discard it. However, a diseased liver does not indicate you cannot eat the muscle tissue.

Cut along each leg from above the foot to the previously made body cut. Remove the hide by pulling it away from the carcass, cutting the connective tissue where necessary. Cut off the head and feet.

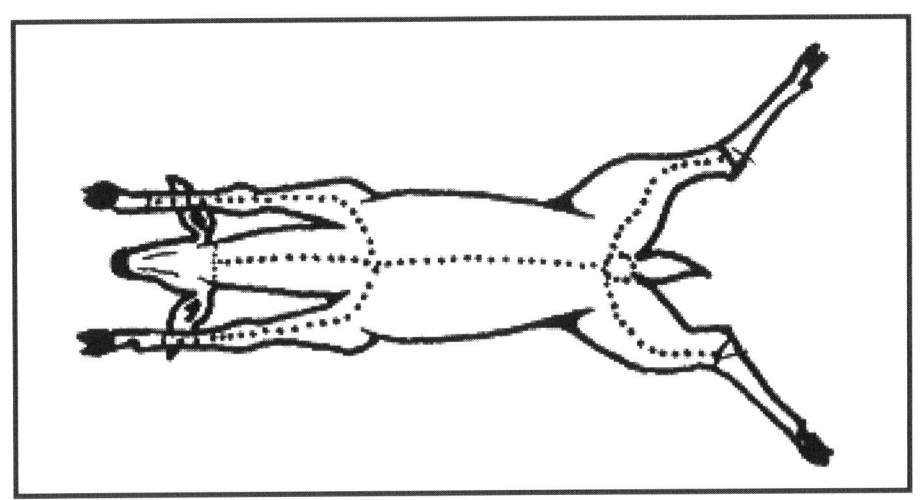

Skinning and Butchering Large Game

Cut larger game into manageable pieces. First, slice the muscle tissue connecting the front legs to the body. There are no bones or joints connecting the front legs to the body on four-legged animals. Cut the hindquarters off where they join the body. You must cut around a large bone at the top of the leg and cut to the ball-and-socket hip joint. Cut the ligaments around the joint and bend it back to separate it. Remove the large muscles (the tenderloin or "backstrap") that lie on either side of the spine. Separate the ribs from the backbone. There is less work and less wear on your knife if you break the ribs first, then cut through the breaks.

Boil large meat pieces or cook them over a spit. You can stew or boil smaller pieces, particularly those that remain attached to bone after the initial butchering, as soup or broth. You can cook body organs such as the heart, liver, pancreas, spleen, and kidneys using the same methods as for muscle meat. You can also cook and eat the brain. Cut out the tongue, skin it, boil it until tender, and eat it.

Smoking Meat

To smoke meat, in a zombie free zone, prepare an enclosure around a fire. Two ponchos snapped together will work. The fire does not need to be big, nor hot. The intent is to produce smoke and heat, not flame. Do not use resinous wood because its smoke will ruin the meat. Use hardwoods to produce good smoke. The wood should be somewhat green. If it is too dry, soak it. Cut the meat into thin slices, no more than about 1/4 inch thick, and drape them over a framework. Make sure none of the meat touches another piece. Keep the poncho enclosure around the meat to hold the smoke and keep a close watch on the fire. Do not let the fire get too hot. Meat smoked overnight in this manner will last about 1 week. Two days of continuous smoking will preserve the meat for 2 to 4 weeks. Properly smoked meat will look like a dark, curled, brittle stick and you can eat it without further cooking. You can also use a pit to smoke meat.

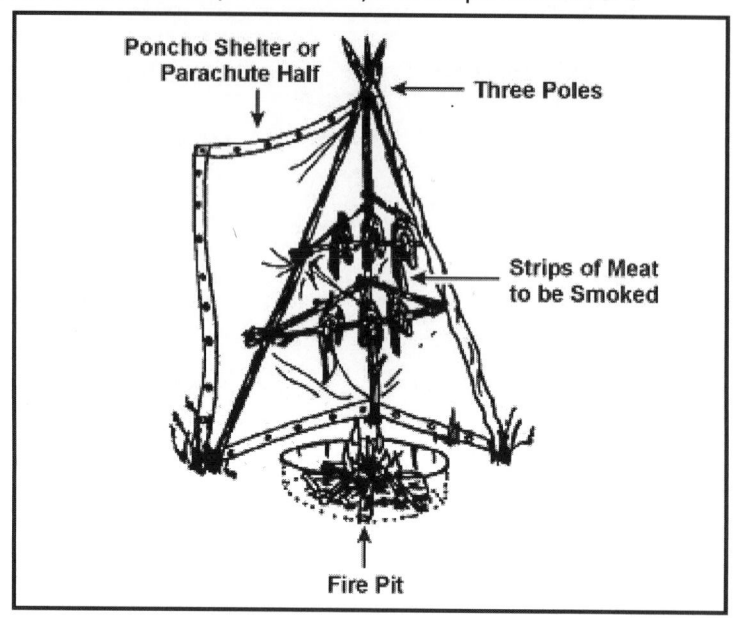

Teepee Smoker

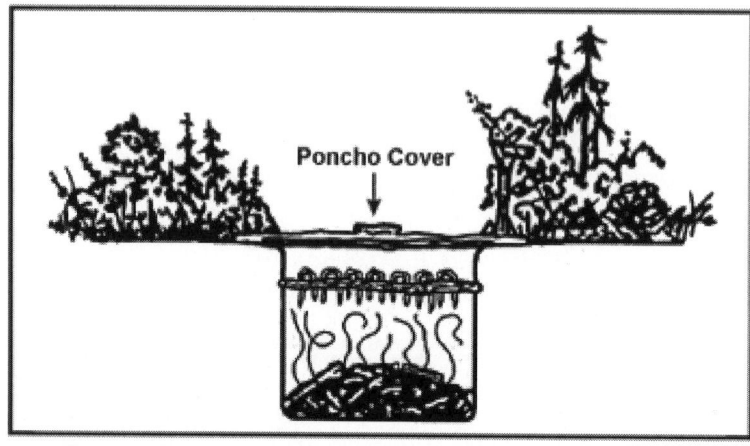

Smoking Meat Over a Pit

Drying Meat

To preserve meat by drying, in a zombie free environment, cut it into 1/4-inch strips with the grain. Hang the meat strips on a rack in a sunny location with good airflow. Keep the strips out of the reach of animals and the hordes of flesh eaters. Cover the strips to keep off blowflies. Allow the meat to dry thoroughly before eating. Properly dried meat will have a dry, crisp texture and will not feel cool to the touch.

Other Preservation Methods

You can also preserve meats using the freezing or brine and salt methods. In cold climates, you can freeze and keep meat indefinitely. Freezing is not a means of preparing meat. You must still cook it before eating. You can also preserve meat by soaking it thoroughly in a saltwater solution. The solution must cover the meat. You can use salt by itself but make sure you wash off the salt before cooking.

PLANTS FOR FOOD

Plants are valuable sources of food because they are widely available, easily procured, and, in the proper combinations, can meet all your nutritional needs. The critical factor in using plants for food is to avoid accidental poisoning. Eat only those plants you can positively identify and you know are safe to eat.

Tasting or swallowing even a small portion of some plants can cause severe discomfort, extreme internal disorders, and even death. Therefore, if you have the slightest doubt about a plant's edibility, apply this Universal Edibility Test before eating any portion of it.

1. Test only one part of a potential food plant at a time.
2. Separate the plant into its basic components—leaves, stems, roots, buds, and flowers.
3. Smell the food for strong or acid odors.
4. Do not eat for 8 hours before starting the test.
5. During the 8 hours you abstain from eating, test for contact poisoning by placing a piece of the plant part you are testing on the inside of your elbow or wrist. Usually 15 minutes is enough time to allow for a reaction.
6. During the test period, take nothing by mouth except purified water and the plant part.
7. Select a small portion of a single part and prepare it the way you plan to eat it.
8. Before placing the prepared plant part in your mouth, touch a small portion to the outer surface of your lip to test for burning or itching.

9. If after 3 minutes there is no reaction on your lip, place the plant part on your tongue, holding it there for 15 minutes.
10. If there is no reaction, chew a pinch and hold it in your mouth for 15 minutes. Do not swallow.
11. If no burning, itching, numbing, stinging, or other irritation occurs during the 15 minutes, swallow the food.
12. Wait 8 hours. If any ill effects occur during this period, induce vomiting and drink a lot of water.
13. If no ill effects occur, eat 0.25 cup of the same plant part prepared the same way. Wait another 8 hours. If no ill effects occur, the plant part, as prepared, is safe for eating.

Test all parts of the plant for edibility, as some plants have both edible and inedible parts. Do not assume that a part that proved edible when cooked is also edible when raw. Test the part raw to ensure edibility before eating raw. The same part or plant may produce varying reactions in different individuals.

To avoid potentially poisonous plants, stay away from any wild or unknown plants that have—

- Milky or discolored sap
- Beans, bulbs, or seeds inside pods
- A bitter or soapy taste
- Spines, fine hairs, or thorns
- Foliage that resembles dill, carrot, parsnip, or parsley
- An almond scent in woody parts and leaves
- Grain heads with pink, purplish, or black spurs
- A three-leafed growth pattern
- Grown near roads

Also, avoid all mushrooms; there is no room for experimentation during a zombie survival situation.

While this is fair guidance for procuring food during the zombie apocalypse, it should be complimented with field guides and hands-on training.

As a result of the zombie apocalypse, civilization as we know it will perish. Using models of pandemics, scientists prove mankind must, without delay, strike back relentlessly to avoid extinction.

Modeling the small zombie outbreaks of today, researchers study the affect of the infectious undead on the living. The conclusion is, to avoid doom, destroying the zombies straightaway is the only method of survival.

The coexistence of the undead and the living is impossible. Eliminate them directly.

8 – Zombie Combat

While the best form of self-defense against a predator that feels no pain, has no faith, and only has eating you mind, is avoidance, confrontation is unavoidable. Understanding zombie weaknesses and arming yourself with the proper tools and training will mean the difference between killing a dangerous rotting sack of bones and guts, and becoming one.

Prepare for the zombie apocalypse by getting a better understanding of the undead's strengths and weaknesses, and our strengths and weaknesses as humans.

UNDERSTANDING ZOMBIE NATURE

One of the more gut-wrenching stories of misunderstanding zombie nature is that of the young Haitian family. In an effort to dissuade her attack, the father used their infant as a bribed attempt to appeal to his newly zombified wife's maternal instincts. After tearing the infant from his arms and devouring a better part of it, she turned her attention to his shocked and cowering body. Understanding zombie nature is a must for survival.

Zombies are in no way the humans they once were. Zombies' one natural instinct is to feed on the living. Their slow, limitless endurance is in pursuit of the target, and the preceding attack is a means to feeding.

Zombie Neurobiology

What is wrong with zombies that make them the stumbling, ravenously hungry corpses they are? Their infected brains, of course.

The undead's cerebellum, located at the bottom back of the brain, is damaged. In a healthy human brain, the cerebellum helps maintain coordination, precision, timing and balance. Non-zombified human brains with cerebellums temporarily affected by alcohol consumption result in humans with poor motor control similar to the effects of ataxia. Ataxia is a disease that causes nervous system damage resulting in poor balance and difficulty walking. Studies of zombified cerebellums reveal similar, but permanent damage.

The undead's orbital frontal cortex, a part of the frontal lobe, is also damaged. In a healthy human brain, the frontal lobe helps recognize and weigh the consequences of actions, to choose between good and bad, and to suppress socially unacceptable behavior. Non-zombified human brains with damaged frontal lobes result in humans with blunted emotions and personality. Studies of zombified frontal lobes reveal no activity. As such, the undead are unable to solve complex problems, and unable to feel pain.

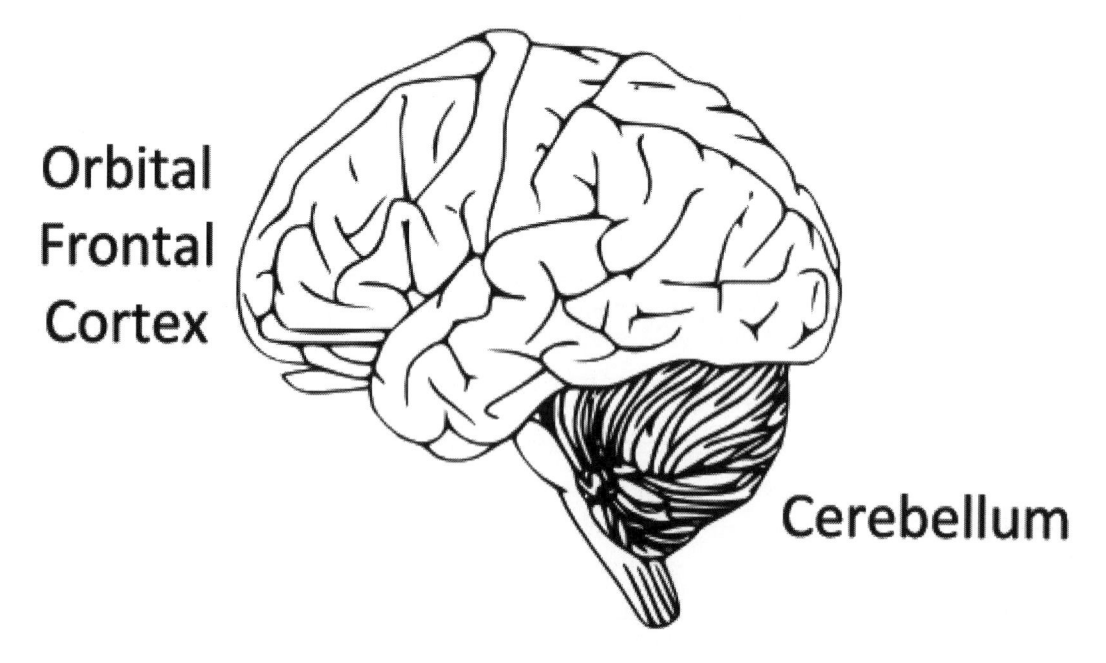

Without the frontal lobe, a zombie's primitive impulse to feed is unhindered by any outside or internal influences.

Zombie Strengths

- Zombies bite.

- The Undead have a death grip like a crocodile.

- Shuffling Aggressors scratch.

- Reanimated spread infection through scratching and biting.

- Soulless Stiffs do not feel pain, responding to gunshots to the chest with only a stumble and resumed attack.

- Animated Cadavers do not tire. Their endurance lasts as long as their brain.

- Reawakened Corpses do not need sleep, nor rest.

- The Dead Warmed Over are not hindered by bodily functions like thirst or having to use the bathroom.

- Flesh Eaters hear and smell their prey with senses keener than the living.

- Unpleasant Undead have supernatural senses. Even without eyes or ears, they are able to track prey.

- Stumbling Remains can function without all of their body. They are Terminator-like in their indestructability, undeterred by the loss of arms or legs.

- Carnivorous Carcasses can survive underwater until their brains rot, as their dead lungs do not require oxygen.

- Decaying Deceased stink like a rotten fridge, expelling noxious fumes capable of disabling humans. The stench, in close quarters, can be so overwhelming that battle hardened soldiers and emergency responders have been known to drop to their knees with the dry heaves. Their stench can also be a liability.

Zombie Weaknesses

- Without an intact brain, zombies are just dead bodies.

- After only a few hours of zombification, the reanimated develop a rotten stench. As with the cucumber smell of a diamondback rattlesnake, catching this scent ahead of time can serve as an early warning system that danger is near. Too close, though, and that stench becomes their asset.

- Zombies are not intelligent. Their actions are not based on learned skills or experiences; they are based solely on the hunger instinct. The infected live for one primary purpose, eating.

- Shuffling corpses move slowly. Even a newly reanimated Olympian Sprinter moves at a maximum 3 miles per hour. Leg injuries, pre- or post-infection, further hinder their speed.

- The carnivorous cadavers cannot resist live flesh. Zombies eat all living animals, not just humans, not just brains.

UNDERSTANDING HUMANS

Now that we have a good grasp on the enemy, let's take a look at ourselves, the human race.

Human strengths:

- Intelligence is the capacity for learning, reasoning, and understanding. An immediate example of your intelligence is that you are making this effort to prepare for the zombie apocalypse.

- In many ways, human bodies are self-healing.

- Infant humans can detect zombies sooner than toddlers, children, or adults. This is most likely because at the earliest stage of development the other senses have not yet overpowered our natural extrasensory perception. Scientific studies show an otherwise content infant, when brought near a zombie, will begin a distinctly sharp cry. Hence the phrase, "Baby butthead? Watch for undead!"

Human weaknesses:

- Humans have nerves that can debilitate their bodies through pain.

- Humans tend to humanize zombies. Mistakenly treating zombies like humans accounts for over half the fatalities in zombie outbreaks. You didn't cause their affliction, you cannot control their affliction, and you cannot cure their affliction without destroying the brain. Allowing personal feelings about the person the zombie once was, gets in the way of survival.

- Humans fear. Nothing, not even this training and desensitization can prepare you for your first zombie encounter. The way they look, the way they smell, the sounds they make, and the danger they represent is frightening beyond even near death experiences.

- Human bodies are easily wounded.

- Human nature is to succumb when put to enough mental stressors.

Applying an understanding of zombie and human strengths and weaknesses will help one to survive the zombie apocalypse.

DECEIVING ZOMBIES

Leveraging the undead's lack of intelligence, you can use basic tactics to direct zombies.

Because even zombies without ears react to noises, using deceptive noises to draw zombies towards a trap, or away from your location, are both valid options. In some situations, strategically placed wind chimes can be used for this purpose.

Because even zombies without noses react to smell, using fresh blood, meat, or sacrificial animals can be used for the same deceptive purposes.

Early measures of zombie deception by military formations included the use of smoke bombs. Do not use smoke bombs to shield your location. Zombie senses are not fooled by a shield of smoke, while human senses are easily overwhelmed by it.

In some instances smoke bombs have been successfully used to attract zombies.

Hordes of Zombies

It is important to understand that zombies do not intentionally gather together. Zombies are the ultimate self-centered loners; concerned only with their next meal. The lure of live flesh, sound, or smell is the concentrating force. They are not communicating, and they do not realize that they are more dangerous in numbers.

And yet, we know from history, experience, and logic that the greater number of zombies in a horde, the more dangerous individual zombies become. Mathematically, the expression is

$$\text{When } n=1 \text{ then } D_z=1, \text{ but when } n>1 \text{ then } D_z=2^{n-1}$$

If n is the number of zombies present in a given horde, and D_z is the potential zombie danger in that environment. The potential danger created by a zombie increases by an order of magnitude with each zombie added. In other words, two zombies may be 2 times as dangerous as one; three may be 4 times as dangerous; four, 8 times as dangerous, and so on.

But do not waste your time doing a headcount until after their brains are dead.

Recognizing this exponential increase in danger with zombie hordes, aside from avoiding them altogether, another approach would be to split the horde and deal with the numbers one division at a time.

Some successful techniques for this include

- Using the lure of sound or bait, funnel the shuffling dead into an elongated space no wider than three feet, where, from an elevated and safe location, you can destroy their brains one at a time. Tight alleyways between buildings, where you can work from an open window or firescape, are well suited for this purpose.

- Splitting a horde using a dividing structure facilitates decreased danger and greater zombie manageability. Fences and garden walls are excellent for this purpose. Using the lure of sound or bait, split the horde to both sides of the dividing structure. Of course, still be prepared to handle both smaller groups, but now with exponentially less danger.

- If the horde is small enough, closed doors can be used to separate zombies. I always love watching this technique, as when done right, it has a comical aspect to it. Using the fastest of your group as bait, guide the horde towards a house that is pre-prepared with open doors from the entryway through the first floor open bathroom window. If given a long enough trail, the fastest of the zombies, still much slower than the typical human being pursued by zombies, will pull away from the horde before the bait reaches the house. Once the bait and all of the breakoff zombies are in the house, an accomplice closes the entry door and the bait crawls out the bathroom window. The rest of the horde, the slower zombies, are dealt with first, then, if there is value to using the house, those in the house are handled in a narrow hallway approach.

Remember: Every zombie removed from a horde decreases the danger of that horde by a negative exponent of 2.

Always practice these techniques on a small scale before trying to implement them on groups of zombies that outnumber your group four to one. Only battle hardened, experienced zombie survivalists should attempt any of these techniques on groups of zombies greater than 40.

PLAN FOR VICTORY

If you cannot avoid the undead altogether, use these five mandates to plan well enough to ensure victory. Keep everyone in your group involved to increase teamwork and safety.

1. Choose the location for the conflict. Knowing where you will be when it happens will help eliminate some unexpected variables while increasing your opportunities for escape.
2. Plan two escape routes with safe bug out locations. Escaping alive is a victory. It is just as good to escape unscathed with zero zombie kills as it is to escape alive with ten zombie kills.
3. Decrease the danger of a horde by dividing it into more manageable groups.
4. Always carry a primary, secondary, and tertiary weapon, including, if required, ammunition.
5. Keep zombies within your reach for killing, while keeping yourself safely out of their reach. If they cannot get to you, and you can still escape to a bug out location, you are doing great.

Objective: Destroy The Brain

Severing a zombie's head is not enough. Severed zombie heads have a reputation of lasting for months in the area around inexperienced extermination areas. Think your single machete swipe was enough? Please save us all the excitement of being attacked at our ankles by taking the time to find the head and destroy the brain.

To stop a zombie, one must destroy the brain. A cursory review of the human skull reveals five sweet spots one should consider targets. Each eye socket is a channel through the skull to the brain. The nasal aperture is another. Under the back of the skull, lies the fourth, and through the roof of the mouth is a fifth.

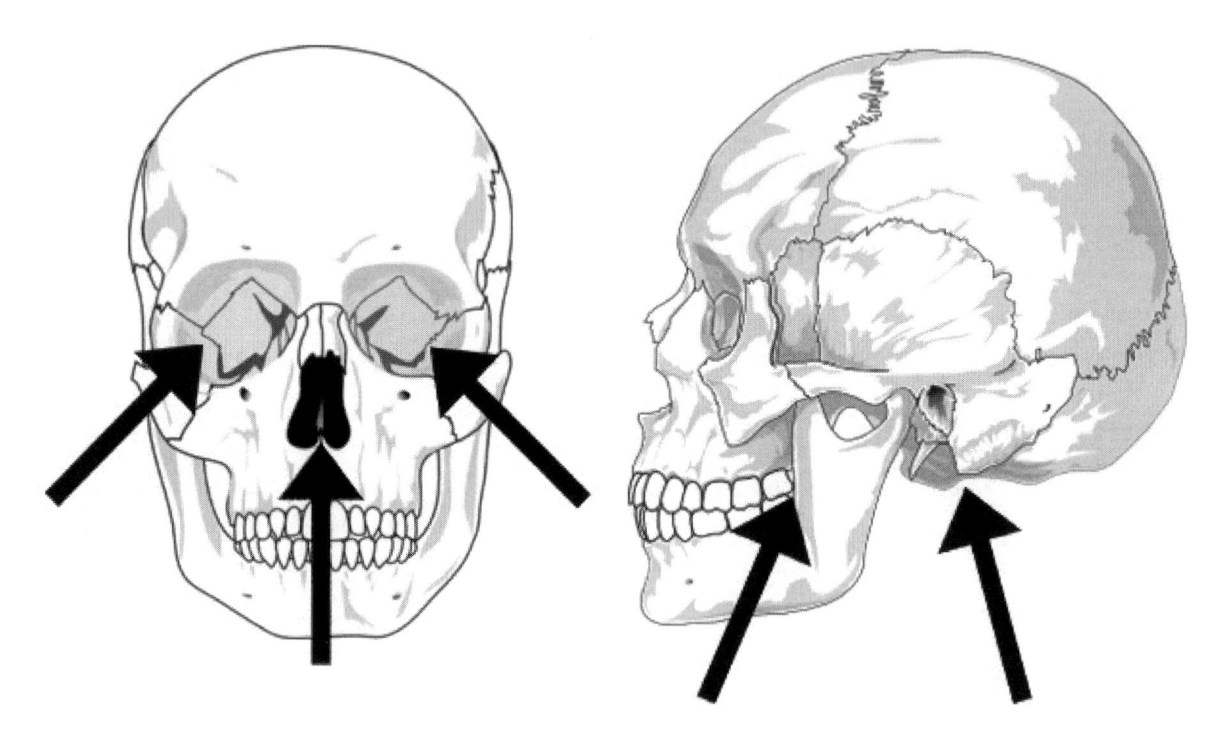

Sport and occupational helmets can be a hindrance in accessing these sweet spots. Practice all five kill shots to give yourself additional options. Without a gun, reconsider engaging a zombie wearing a full face motorcycle helmet.

Horrors Of Zombie Combat

Fighting a global war against the undead will be unlike any combat situation in history. An ever aggressive enemy that does not feel pain, and is not afraid of anything, will plunge humankind into horrors of killing or being killed. Few of the living will be battle-hardened zombie combat veterans with honed skills. The majority of survivalists will be inexperienced and young. Many will manage to cope well enough in these immensely difficult conditions, but some will not. Zombie combat fatigue will be a common ailment, especially for those involved in areas of high zombie activity. Prepare for the horrors of combat with the reanimated; know what to expect.

You will witness many of your loved ones dying, becoming zombified, or both. Take the time to grieve, when you can, but recognize that the ones who die actually fare better than the zombified. You may find yourself having to destroy the infected brain of a loved one.

The best advice for dealing with the horrors of a zombified loved one is three-fold. First, act quickly. Any hesitation can lead to the death of yourself or others. There is no benefit to prolonging exposure to the shuffling flesh eaters, even if you were once related. Second, do not make eye contact. This applies to all zombies. By doing so, your mind may try to draw connections between the reanimated flesh eater and the human they once were. The undead are not the humans they once were. Third, recognize zombie euthanasia as a good deed. They are already dead; you are simply putting them to rest.

For the zombie survivalist who cannot destroy the infected brain of a loved one, flesh eating infants, zombified children, or undead elderly, containment is an option. Remember, though, that no containment is permanent due to the tenacity of zombies.

If you become infected, present a copy of your **Advance Directive for an Unnatural Death ("Undead Will"), then** consider the option of making best use of yourself before you turn. The fleeting moments after becoming infected, but before becoming a zombie, is a short period of time where one can immerse themselves in zombie dispatching without the fear of uncertainty. As the infected living, if you are able to destroy the brains of only two zombies, then the world is one zombie safer than before. Without fear of becoming infected, abandoning the hope of living in a zombie-free world will allow you to reduce the undead risk to your fellow zombie survivalists. There is no benefit to accelerating your death through suicide, nor through only excommunicating yourself from the group. Quickly fulfill your last emotional, spiritual, and mental wishes, then go save some lives by fearlessly mingling with, and destroying the brains, of the undead!

Zombie Combat Dress

As important as weapons, defensive clothing saves lives during zombie combat. Dress for success. Short hair and tight clothes decrease the opportunity for the undead's grasp and entanglement in objects like chain-link fences, branches, and car doors. Fancy hairdos and makeup are pre-zombie-apocalyptic niceties; your new attractiveness will be your ability to survive. Staying clean helps a survivalist stay healthy.

Generally speaking, a zombie survivalist should wear durable, lightweight, tightfitting clothing with enough pockets to carry necessities and a fit that allows a full range of motion.

In the event of a physical zombie attack, you will be glad you are wearing long pants and any other protective gear. Because full coverage is desirable, gloves are a must. At times, armored clothing like adventure touring motorcycle gear and riot gear are reasonable approaches.

Dressing in layers is both a smart way to control body temperature, and provides greater protection from zombie bites and scratches. Bruises are better than bites.

Full boots provide real protection to your feet that shoes cannot. A boot's ankle support and bite suppression are immediate benefits. Their unlikeliness of slipping off when the going gets tough is another. A zombie survivalist must take care of their feet.

There may be times when a protective exoskeleton created by the addition of a full helmet, elbow, knee, and wrist pads, gloves, and high reaching boots will give you a feeling of zinvincibility. Do not be fooled by your clothing altered ego; a zombie's grip will work just as well on any of those pieces of clothing as it would your bare arm, and the grip may not be released until the zombie is destroyed.

WEAPONS

Contrary to your braggadocios friends, there is not one weapon BEST for killing a zombie. Different weapons are best suitable at different times for different survivalists. Always carry primary, secondary, and tertiary weapons, including, if required, ammunition.

Weapons you choose should be practiced with to perfection. You do not want to be learning to wield a mace during the chaos and panic of a zombie fight. Hell, you do not want to wield a mace at all during a zombie fight! Pick an appropriate weapon.

Inappropriate Weapons

Hand to Hand Combat

A word on hand to hand combat with a zombie. Don't.

If you accidentally get into hand to hand combat with a zombie, do all you can to deflect the advancing hands and mouth, then, run away. Immediately afterwards, seek medical attention. Have a trained medical professional examine you for scratches or bites, even if you do not feel any. The zombie virus doesn't require much of an entry, and you do not want to put the others in your group in danger. Knowing you have become infected at the earliest opportunity will allow you to make the smartest decisions about getting your house in order.

Heavy or Bulky

Inappropriate zombie killing weapons include weapons that are too heavy to carry on long hikes or too bulky to carry without a motorized vehicle. It is true that high caliber assault rifles are well suited for human combat, where every landed shot slows an enemy, but try carrying one such rifle and one hundred rounds of ammunition (only about 15 combined pounds) for a ten mile hike, and you will get a good understanding of why military combat personnel constantly train.

Clobbering

While everyone thinks they can use a weapon that clobbers, from baseball bats to tree branches to thrown bricks, you will be surprised to find how ineffective they are against a zombie. While cool to look at, the bar mace is inappropriate for killing zombies. The undead feel about as much pain as the dead; none. Do not weigh yourself down with ineffective weaponry.

Onetime Use

Some weapons can only be relied upon to be used once. Weapons like the machete, axe, hatchet, pitchfork, ice climbing pick, and crowbar are certainly able to land a zombie brain piercing blow, but history shows that, in the hands of the inexperienced, they are often one time use weapons because they become lodged in the skull. Yes, the zombie is dead, but now it is also dead weight attached to the end of your weapon, leaving you weaponless and susceptible to attack by the next zombie.

Overkill Guns

Contrary to your gut feeling about the matter, not all guns are well suited for zombie killing. Shotguns are so loud they attract more zombies, weigh so much they are tough to tote, and the ammunition is so bulky it limits the rounds one can carry. Additionally, many shotgun rounds have a spreading effect when fired, and are ill suited for piercing the skull to kill the brain, except at close distance. Many assault rifles, like the ever popular AR-15 and SKS models, also require heavy and bulky ammunition with a caliber larger than necessary to dispatch the undead. To further put guns into a perspective, every gun needs bullets. Unless you have prepared appropriately, you are bound to eventually run out of bullets, rendering the gun down to the level of a clobbering weapon. Some guns though, in rightly trained hands, can certainly help one survive the zombie apocalypse.

Appropriate Weapons

Pick a weapon that is appropriate for you.

Tertiary Weaponry

For your tertiary weapon, consider a close range puncturing tool. Good for close quarter confrontations, in the skilled hand, a puncturing weapon can be beautifully effective. As some slaughter houses can attest, a spike to the just the right spot in the brain can drop a zombie like a slaughtered cow. Learning this skill takes the right weapon and lots of practice.

In the history of mankind, a good stout blade has been the weapon of choice. Bowie, Rambo-type survival knives, Ka-bar knives, or even bayonets suffice. Long bladed screwdrivers and ice picks are improvised brain puncturing tools. Other suggestions are a Roman Gladius, large meat cleaver, or smatchete.

When it comes down to an in-your-face encounter with a zombie, blades are the long term solution, as all guns will eventually run out of ammunition. Consider a puncturing blade for your tertiary weapon.

Secondary Weaponry

For your secondary weapon, consider a short range piercing tool. Katanas, much smaller and lighter than bulky and heavy long swords, are well suited for not too close zombie combat. A short spear, while not the easiest to tote everywhere, can also be an effective short range piercing tool.

A quality axe with a fiberglass handle can be light weight, and doubles as a hammering and chopping tool. A quality machete can, too. Some other suggestions are the kukri and the crovel.

Remember though, that any blade should not have serrated edges, nor be designed in such a fashion as to become lodged in a zombie's skull. This is meant to be your secondary weapon, not a onetime use weapon, so practice with skulls before using it in the real world of zombie combat.

Primary Weaponry

For your primary weapon, consider a long rang piercing tool. Long range, but quiet guns are well suited as the first line of defense. A small caliber rifle like the popular Ruger 10/22 with scope are exceptionally well suited to pick off advancing zombies far enough away that their minimal sound, small bullets, prolific source of ammunition, and light weight make for an excellent primary weapon. While guns are heavier and louder than other weapons, a zombie survivalist can carry more bullets than arrows, and guns keep the zombies further away.

Both the bow and crossbow are wonderfully silent, so preferable in areas of high zombie concentration. Both have reusable ammunition, and a miss will not reveal the shooter's location. And, unlike a 15 round magazine, a single shot with a bow or crossbow requires the user to take the time to get the shot right the first time.

A zombie survivalist rarely goes wrong when using a gun or bow as their primary weapon.

Dogs as Weapons

Using dogs in times of zombie outbreaks has a long history. Larger dogs have been trained and used for direct combat, useful when clearing houses of individual shuffling undead. Dogs have been used as scouts to identify flesh eaters lurking along trails. Dogs can be trained to serve as sentries, allowing the trainer to sleep, knowing they'll be alerted if the reanimated stumble near. Some dogs can be trained to track the undead. Training a dog takes a lot of time; start now to ensure your four legged friend has a fighting chance at surviving the zombie apocalypse.

Additional Comments About Weapons

- Train. Train. Train. No weapon is effective in the hands of an unskilled user. Online you will find many zombie killing weapons. Evaluate each by what you have learned here. Pick the lightest weight, least bulky solution that fits your personality and ability, and start practicing.

- Practice with your weapons, in life like situations, no less than monthly.

- Every gun is only as good as the ammunition lasts.

- A wrist strap is always nice. Things get dicey during zombie combat, and it is easy to lose your grip.

- Never give a weapon to someone you do not trust.

- After your primary, secondary, and tertiary weapons, do not lose your life because you didn't improvise. If there is something within arm's reach that will do the job of piercing a zombies skull and killing its brain, try to use it.

Avoidance

The greatest form of zombie self-defense is Avoidance. Learn to move defensively in zombie occupied areas.

The zombie apocalypse will wreak havoc on transportation and mobility. As society falls into disorder, roads and sidewalks will become impassable due to wrecked and deserted vehicles. Doorways, hallways, and stairwells will be littered with items we once used for everyday life. In the maddened flight for life, most personal belongings will be simply abandoned.

The routine traffic of life as we now experience it will be replaced by random frightened people just trying to find life enabling resources, moving through a chain of temporarily safe positions. Fear will be justified by the ever present, relentless undead corpses tracking, wandering, and searching for the next opportunity to feed on the living.

A task as simple as feeding a group of people will require great effort. Food, scarcer by the day, will require dangerous passage through zombie infested areas. Successful movement through zombie infested areas will require skill, patience, strength, endurance, and planning.

9 - SURVIVAL MOVEMENT IN ZOMBIE INFESTED AREAS

Movement is the secondary fault for drawing a zombie's attention, preceded by noise and followed by scent. Zombies sense movement through what seems to be a form of sonar or telepathy. Some scientists believe the infected brain accesses a sense tied to the ethereal continuum. Whatever the explanation, even zombies missing eyes sense movement.

The key rules for survival movement in zombie infested areas are

- Always move when in imminent danger
- Otherwise, only move with a planned purpose
- Move with intentional milestones – smart location to smart location
- Move to avoid, not engage, the undead

AVOIDANCE

The greatest form of zombie self-defense is Avoidance.

It is unlikely, though, to be able to completely avoid all zombies throughout your entire survival efforts. Survivors of the zombie apocalypse will have to move in areas of zombie infestation to gather food, supplies, water, and to avoid the shuffling hordes. As such, let's look at methods to avoid zombies, realistically.

Noise Avoidance

Quiet! Noise is the primary fault for drawing a zombie's attention. Discipline and a little attention to detail can mean the difference between avoiding an encounter and serving yourself to the flesh eaters. Intentional noises like shotgun blasts should be avoided, but also avoid music from headphones, the clunky grind of a rusty bicycle chain, slamming doors, a squeaky boot, the sound of footsteps in the woods, even down to the tink-tink-tink of your machete handle against your belt.

Children in your group? It is imperative to start teaching them at the earliest possible day to avoid making noise on the cue of an adult. Any parent will tell you how tough that is during these non-zombie-apocalyptic times, but rest assured that the seriousness of the matter will result in quieter children when it becomes a life or death situation. Unfortunately, childhood, for the children reared during a zombie outbreak, is filled with imminent danger forcing a faster maturation. Keeping newborns through toddlers quiet during a brush with the undead is one of the toughest challenges you will encounter. Due to a baby's unpredictability, in case the crying child attracts the undead, you must always be ready to defend yourself, while protecting the child. Remember that infant humans can detect zombies sooner than toddlers, children, or adults. Baby butthead? Watch for undead! As it is with potty training, one day, the child will reach the milestone of sensing the discomfort of a zombie encounter and start practicing a defensive silence.

Only well trained dogs should accompany your survivalist group. Training a dog to not instinctively bark at the undead takes time, attention, and practice. Use praise or reward when your dog follows your signal to keep quiet near zombies.

When moving in zombie infested areas, noise is a killer and must be avoided.

Hand Signals

Shut up when you are talking to me.

Hand signals are the smart solution for silent communication. Following the standardized set in Appendix C, adapted from the Standardized Hand Signals for Close Range Engagement (C.R.E.) Operations, will allow easy integration of other survivalists to your group, and you to theirs. When communicating via hand signals, everyone in the immediate group should repeat the signal as recognition of successful communication.

Smell

Take the time to smell the roses. Do they smell like rotting flesh? You may be downwind from one or more zombies. Consider leaving the area, but always have a solid plan for your next stop.

Modes of Transportation

During the zombie apocalypse, human powered modes of transportation like walking, hiking, and bicycling will be the most reliable and longest lasting. Because they rely heavily on your personal strength and energy, start training now to prepare your body and mind for the requirements of walking 10 miles per day, hiking 5 miles per day, and bicycling 50 miles per day.

The use of pack animals like horses, mules, camel, or llamas is not recommended. Like you, they are live flesh, zombie magnets. Unlike you, they react to the presence of a zombie with unpredictable panic. You do not want to lose your ammunition and food supplies because your donkey was spooked by an undead flesh eater.

Motorcycles are fuel efficient and able to go places wider, less maneuverable vehicles cannot. During the early days of the apocalypse, skilled riders on motorcycles and scooters will be able to maneuver through the traffic jams that leave others stranded and susceptible to the oncoming horde of shuffling undead. While the lack of a motorcycle endorsement will not matter during this period of mass hysteria and unrest, experience with starting, controlling, and stopping a motorized two wheeler may save your life.

Common misperception is that Hummers and large 4x4 trucks will serve their owners well during the zombie apocalypse. That is agreeable, but only for the first tank of gas. In the long run, without gas and a mechanic, these machines will falter to the scarcity of fuel and mechanical failure from off road use.

When to Move

In most situations, during the zombie apocalypse, hide during the night and move during the day. Travelling at night puts you at a disadvantage. The undead do not need light to sense movement, but you do.

On hot days, try to limit your travel to the cooler morning and evening temperatures. Your energy and water supply will last longer.

Travelling in areas of ice and snow has its benefits. The undead lack metabolism and the heat it generates. In freezing temperatures, a zombie's body freezes to the point of immobility within hours. Blizzards and cold winds do not mean freezing temperatures; avoid poor visibility weather unless you are in imminent danger otherwise.

Consider water travel when applicable, but security from the undead is not as easy as avoiding the shore. Do not put all your faith in personal floatation devices when crossing water. While zombies do not swim, they also do not breathe. A life jacket will not protect you from a submerged zombie's reach. Zombies from outbreaks miles away have surfaced, undead and threatening, miles downstream from their last sighting.

When you can, move slowly, stopping to look, listen, and smell. The upper torso of the undead can lay for months in tall grass, brush, swamps, and water. It only takes one scratch to become infected. Survivors of zombie outbreaks recall literally stumbling upon severed undead heads, still biting at the ankles of passersby.

PLANNING

Preparation is a requirement before any movement in zombie infested areas. When planning, you must consider how to avoid zombies and get to the next safe environment. Evasion plans must be prepared in conjunction with everyone in your group. It is unacceptable to lose human life to mistakes made when moving through zombie infested areas. Establish backup plans and escape routes for all members in your group.

Zombie Avoidance Plan of Action

Successful zombie avoidance requires effective prior planning. The responsibility ultimately rests on the individual concerned. Sound zombie avoidance planning should incorporate intelligence briefings—selected areas for avoidance, survey descriptions, personnel reports, and an avoidance plan of action.

The study and research needed to develop avoidance planning will make you aware of the current zombie situation in your area. Your planning must let every member of your group know your probable actions should you have to move to avoid the undead.

Start preparing even before the zombie apocalypse begins. Include zombie avoidance in your training. Planning starts in your daily training.

Standing Avoidance Procedure

Your group's standing avoidance procedures are valuable tools that will help plan movement in zombie infested areas. The time to discuss options is not when faced with a dangerous situation requiring immediate action. Items your group should agree upon should include, but are not limited to—

- Movement team size (two to four persons per team)
- Team communications
- Essential equipment
- Actions at danger areas
- Signaling techniques
- Immediate action drills
- Defensive security procedures during movement and at hide sites
- Rally points

Rehearsals work effectively for reinforcing avoidance skills and also provide opportunities for evaluation and improvement.

MOVING

Upon realization of zombie infestation, all moving team members will try to link up at a rally point. The rally point is where team members gather to begin the group movement. Tentatively select the point during your planning phase through reconnaissance. Everyone in your group must know the location. The rally point should be easy to locate and occupy for a minimum amount of time.

Once the group has rallied at the point, it must—

- Give first aid.
- Inventory equipment (decide what to abandon, or take along).
- Make sure everyone knows the tentative hide locations.
- Ensure everyone knows the primary and alternate routes and rally points en route to the hide locations.
- Always maintain security.
- Split the team into smaller elements. The ideal element should have two to four members; however, it could include more depending on team equipment and experience.

The movement portion of passing through zombie infested areas is the most dangerous, as you are then most vulnerable. It is usually better to move during the day because of the concealment darkness offers the undead, and the hindrance it gives humans. When moving, avoid the following even if it takes more time and energy to bypass:

- Obstacles and barriers
- Cities and towns
- Areas of high zombie population

Pick your terrain wisely. While zombies find even the shortest of fences difficult to overcome, they'll walk across hot coals with a greater determination than a student of Tony Robbins.

Movement in zombie-infested territory is a very deliberate process. At times, the slower you move and the more careful you are, the greater your chances of survival. Your best security will be using your senses. Use your eyes and ears to detect the undead before they detect you. Make frequent listening halts. In daylight, observe a section of your route before you move along it. The distance you travel before you hide will depend on the zombie situation, your health, the terrain, the availability of defendable space, and the amount of daylight left.

Once you have moved into the area in which you want to hide, select a bug out site. Keep the word SHED in mind when selecting a hide site:

- S – Sized for the Group
- H – High Observation
- E – Exits (Multiple)
- D – Defendable

Usually, your worst option will be to crawl into thick vegetation. Setting up a tent takes time, leaves you exposed to the first mindless undead to stumble into the campsite, and typically leaves you with only one way in or out. Think a high hung hammock or tree stand makes sense? You will be thinking again four days later when the growing horde of undead below prove they can outlast your need for water and food.

Hospitals, Police Stations, and Public Emergency Shelters also make for undesirable bug out locations. During the early days of the apocalypse, these locations will be flooded with the living and the infected. These locations will become the veritable breeding ground for the fall of civilization. It will take years for most of these locations to become suitable for occupation by the living.

Use the houses, buildings, and existing shelters you find along the way. In addition to the route you took into the building, always have two escape routes. There is nothing wrong with sleeping in a car if the car is operable and you have two routes to drive away.

If you must build a shelter, follow the SHED formula.

ACTIVITIES BETWEEN MOVES

After locating your bug out site, do not move straight into it. Conduct a listening halt before entering individually. Be careful not to make noise clearing a pathway. Once occupying the bug out site, limit your activities to maintaining security, resting, and planning your next moves.

Maintain security through visual scanning and listening. Upon detection of the undead, the security personnel alert all personnel, even if the group's plan is to hide and not move upon sighting the undead. Take this action so everyone is aware of the danger and ready to react.

It is extremely important to stay healthy and alert when trying to avoid the undead. Take every opportunity to rest, but do not sacrifice security. Rotate security so that all members in the group can rest. Treat all injuries, no matter how minor. Loss of your health will mean loss of your ability to continue to avoid the invading flesh eaters.

Plan your next actions immediately upon occupying the bug out site. Inform all team members of their current location and designate an alternate bug out site. Once this is done, start planning for the team's next movement.

Planning the team's movement begins with reconnaissance. Choose the next bug out area first. Then choose a primary and an alternate route to the bug out area. In choosing the routes, consider the benefits of not using straight lines. Pick the routes that offer the best cover and concealment, the fewest obstacles, and the least likelihood of contact with zombies. There should be locations along the route where the team can get water. To aid team navigation, use direction, distances, checkpoints or steering marks, and corridors. Plan defendable rally and rendezvous points at intervals along the route.

Other planning considerations are immediate action drills, actions on sighting the undead, and standardized hand-and-arm signals.

Once planning is complete, ensure everyone knows and memorizes the entire plan. The team members should know the distances for the entire route to the next bug out site. They should know the various terrains they will be moving across so that they can move without hesitation.

Limit your actions in the bug out site to those discussed above. Once in the bug out site, restrict all movement to out of sight areas. Do not build fires or prepare food. Smoke and food odors will attract the flesh eaters.

Before leaving the bug out site, leave information for other survivalists. Include such information as the number of members in your group, where your group came from, the location of supply stashes you left behind, and where your group is going.

HOLE-UP AREAS

After moving and hiding for several days, your group will need to move into a hole-up area. This is an area where you can rest, recuperate, and get and prepare food. Choose an area near a water source. You then have a place to get water, to place fishing devices, and to trap game. Since waterways are a line of communication for the living, locate your hole-up site near the water.

The hole-up area should offer plenty of defenses and concealment for movement in and around the area. Always maintain security while in the hole-up area. Always staff the hole-up area. Actions in the hole-up area are the same as in the bug out site, except that you can move away from the hole-up area to get and prepare food. While in the hole-up area, you can—

- Select and occupy the next bug out site.
- Check the area for resources and concealed routes to the alternate bug out site.
- Gather food (nuts, berries, vegetables). When moving around the area for food, maintain security. When setting traps and snares, keep them in areas where other living are not likely to trip them.
- Get water from sources within the hole-up area. Moving on flat rocks or solid ground along the banks to get water will reduce the likelihood of injury.
- Set clandestine fishing devices, such as stakeouts, to avoid noise.
- Locate a fire site away from the hole-up site. Use this site to prepare food or boil water. Be careful that smoke and light from the fire does not compromise the hole-up area.

While in the hole-up area, security is still your primary concern. Designate team members to perform specific tasks. Limit movement around the area, by having a two-person team perform more than one task. For example, the team getting water could also set the fishing devices.

RETURNING TO GREATER NUMBERS

Establishing contact with other survivalists is a crucial part of retreating to areas controlled by the living. All your patience, planning, and hardships will be in vain if you do not exercise caution when contacting other zombie survivalists. Survivalists have killed other survivalists operating in infected areas because they did not make contact properly. Most of the casualties could have been avoided if caution had been exercised and a few simple procedures followed. The normal tendency is to throw caution to the wind when in sight of other groups of living. You must overcome this tendency and understand that joining forces is a very sensitive situation.

Linking Up

If you have made your way to a friendly area, use the following procedures to cross the border and link up with other zombie survivalists:

- Occupy a hide site on the near side of the border and send a team to survey the potential crossing site.

- Survey the crossing site for at least 24 hours, depending on the zombie situation.

- Make a sketch of the site, taking note of terrain, obstacles, and any of the other survivalist group's defensive devices or trip wires. Once the reconnaissance is complete, the team moves to the hole-up site, briefs the rest of the group, and plans to cross the border during daylight.

- After crossing the border, set up a hide site on the far side of the border and try to locate other survivalist positions. Do not reveal your presence.

- Depending on the size of your movement team, have two members survey the potential linkup site until satisfied that the other survivalist group is indeed friendly.

- Make contact with the friendly survivalists during daylight. Personnel chosen to make contact should be unarmed, have no equipment, and have positive identification readily available. The person who actually makes the linkup should be someone who does not look like a zombie and is least threatening.

- During the actual contact, have only one person make the contact. The other person provides the security and observes the link-up area from a safe distance. The observer should be far enough away so that they can warn the rest of the group if something goes wrong.

- Wait until the party being contacted looks in your direction so that you do not surprise the contact. Stand up from behind cover, with hands overhead and state that you are a survivalist. After this, follow any instructions given. Avoid answering any tactical questions and do not give any indication that there are other team members.

- Reveal that there are other personnel only after verifying your identity and satisfying you made contact with friendly forces.

Language problems or difficulties confirming identities may arise. The movement team should maintain security, be patient, and have a contingency plan.

NOTE: If you are moving to an area controlled by the living, you are surrendering to that power and become a humbled servant to the greater good of the accepting group.

The zombie apocalypse will return civilization to a more primitive lifestyle. For many years, some will live without the power, water, sewer, and communication infrastructure we take for granted. Bartering will replace money. Our new lives will require considerable manual labor. Personal farming, ranching, fishing, and hunting will become our primary sources of food. Producing related goods or services will help survivalists barter for other long term supplies. It will take longer than a lifetime for civilization to return to the technology we enjoy today.

Many zombie survivalists lucky enough to avoid death at the hands of the undead will still slowly perish because they will be unable to provide for their own basic needs. Lack of proper nutrition, an inability to deal with stress, and sleep deprivation will lead to poor decisions and the eventual unwillingness to survive.

Planning ahead is the key to having a long term zombie survival solution that includes sustainable water, food, medical support, and a defendable place to live. Do not make the mistake of concentrating only on surviving the initial outbreak; plan and prepare for your long term survival.

10 – LONG TERM SURVIVAL SOLUTIONS

RETREAT SITE SELECTION

The most important factor when choosing your long term zombie apocalypse survival retreat is location, location, location. In choosing the location, consider this proven insight.

Defendable compounds like military bases and prisons are ready made solutions for long term survival of the zombie apocalypse. Clearly delineated borders between acceptable and unacceptable areas of zombie occupation are already established. Moving in, sanitizing the areas inside the fences or walls, then defending these boarders is much easier than starting from scratch with an open campus. Limitations include your inability to own, control, or prepare the site ahead of the outbreak.

Islands seem like a great idea, but zombies are known to traverse water in chase of prey, or randomly arrive on shores due to currents. Being on an island, surrounded by water, is not defense enough from the undead. Added measures of fences and perimeter defense are necessary.

Boats and ships have both assets and limitations for use as long term zombie apocalypse survival sites. Floating in water, they are less susceptible to perimeter breaches by the undead. Sitting above a large, generally flat plane of water, boats and ships provide excellent visibility to approaching dangers like floating flesh eaters. The mobility of the whole site is also an asset. Limitations include limited access to water purification, the necessity of an experienced captain and mechanic, and, in some cases, the requirement for fuel.

Retired military silos are rare and require considerable preparation. The zombie apocalypse will not bring with it the same dangers as a nuclear mishap or foreign enemy attack. When considering a zombie threat, surviving underground requires additional, unnecessary preparation. If using a missile silo as your long term survival retreat, prepare multiple exits.

The typical residential house is not well suited as a long term zombie apocalypse survival retreat. Residential grade fences are not very sturdy and usually do not have securable gates. Most residential houses have many ground level windows. Every window poses a potential point of entry for the undead. Water and food supplies are limited to what is within the house at the time of zombie presence. Residential houses are well suited for the initial 7 days, but not for long term.

General considerations when selecting your retreat location should include:

- an elevated view for long range surveillance
- open surroundings, making approaching hordes of the undead more easily detected
- an area away from densely populated areas, as a lesser population means less potential for zombies

Start camping in the prospective area now to get a sense of the property and local people.

Own the property now, if you can afford it. Document the legal arrangement now. Once the outbreak starts, legal documents will be worthless, but during the preparation and design of the location, everyone should have well-defined rights and roles. Buying adjoining properties with individual ownership makes the most sense. Plus, it creates stickiness to the commitment and dynamics of your group, ensuring everyone has a financial investment.

Site Amenities

In addition to location, the following are desirable site amenities.

- A source of fresh water frees resources otherwise dedicated to procurement and purification. Hand pump wells, springs, and streams are beneficial long term site amenities.

- Freezing temperatures, ice, and snow are exceptionally effective zombie barriers. Due to the lack of heat normally generated from metabolism, zombie bodies freeze quickly. Frozen zombies are harmless, so take the time to eliminate the threats before they thaw.

- Farmable soil is preferred. Plan four acres per person. Consider what food you will be growing, and start planting regular rotations of crops now. Additionally, plant fruit trees. Be prepared in case it happens tomorrow.

- Property immediately next to federal and state parks helps expand the usable footprint beyond property lines.

- Forested areas are preferred. Trees are the smartest source of building material and fuel. Check your neighbors' logging intentions to determine any affects it may have on your long term site selection.

- A hearty wildlife population is a good sign of a healthy environment. Wildlife is food.

- Close proximity to large food storage houses like canned food manufacturers and grain silos helps support easy food procurement.

RETREAT LAYOUT

As you are evaluating a site's strategic location and amenities, you must also evaluate the lay of the land. The proper balance and positioning of defenses, water and food procurement, and waste disposal are at the core of the retreat layout.

Defenses should include a combination of trenches, walls, fences, exits, and maybe towers. As the outer perimeter to the retreat, narrow trenches, dug about knee deep, will drastically slow the advancement of the undead, allowing survivalists at watch to deal with the small problems before they become catastrophic. Narrow, elevated paths through the ditches will allow easy human passage through the same area. An abatis, a defensive obstacle made of outwardly pointed logs and branches, is particularly effective against the undead. Walls and fences serve to delineate the borders between acceptable and unacceptable areas of zombie occupation. They also serve as psychological barriers for survivalists, creating a sense of security within the retreat. Multiple exits, and the training to use them, can save lives should the retreat become overrun with the flesh eating hordes. Towers are nice touch for elevated security from the undead, and greater defensive observation.

The procurement of water and food should be supported by the retreat layout. Positioning a fresh water source within the trenches, walls, and fences will eliminate the resources and risk of leaving the retreat for this necessity. Retreats large enough to hunt within the defenses are rare, but positioning the retreat near hunting grounds or fishing areas is a good idea. Livestock should be positioned downstream to avoid tainting any water source. Small ponds can be used to store live fish within the retreat. Farmlands need not be within the retreat defenses, but not so far away as to create prolonged exposure to zombie attacks. Drying and curing meat will create a smell that will attract the undead. A curing hut within the retreat will provide greater sanitation to the process, but, an elevated area far enough outside the retreat will improve zombie avoidance while still protecting the meat.

Retreat waste falls into three categories: human waste, trash, and dead zombies. Human waste can quickly become a problem for occupants. Basic latrines should be constructed to prevent water contamination and nuisance. Locate the latrines away from any natural water source and at least 100 yards downwind and downhill from the retreat. Devices for washing hands, located at least 10 feet away from the latrines, must be used. The basis for the latrine should be a three foot hole. The hole should be considered full when one foot from ground level. Compacted dirt should be used to fill the hole, and another foot of compacted dirt on top should be used to prevent fly pupae from hatching and gaining access to the open air. Most trash should be burned as fuel and the resulting ashes can be used in composting to create nutrient rich soil. Aluminum cans, plastic bottles, and plastic wrap should be recycled for other uses. Bodies of the undead should be carefully handled and thoroughly incinerated far from the retreat, downhill, downwind, and away from any areas of natural water.

Properly designed zombie apocalypse retreats will defend survivalists from the undead, promote access to useful resources, and prevent disease.

RETREAT SUPPLIES

Unlike zombie survival kits, supplies for a zombie apocalypse retreat are not limited to what you can comfortably carry or fit in your home. Start now, and maybe, through a few trips, you will be lucky enough to fill the retreat with enough hand and farming tools, dried food and spices, playing cards and board games, weapons and ammunition, and all the comforts you can afford for long term survival. Every prepper website has a list. Refer to them and pick what fits your situation.

MOVING DAY AND BEYOND

When you have survived the initial outbreak by staying put for 7 days, when the mass hysteria of looting has passed, and when the hordes of walking corpses begin to stabilize in numbers, it is time to move from your initial bug out location to your previously prepped long term zombie survival retreat.

This move can go smoother by following these few rules.

- Maintain confidence, recognizing that you have planned and trained for this move.
- Do not take shortcuts. Keep to your plan.
- Pack only the food, water, weapons and supplies you will need for the trip, or that you do not have waiting at your retreat.
- Stash remaining supplies, but leave a note of their whereabouts for other zombie survivalists.
- Avoid the zombies, even if it means a slower move.
- Thoroughly sanitize the long term site of all zombie activity, establishing defensive barriers as you go.
- Maintain a high defensive position for the first 30 days.

Never let down your guard, but do relax knowing you have done your preparation and proven your long term survivability.

BEGINNING YOUR ZOMBIE PREPAREDNESS JOURNEY

Every survivalist's journey through the zombie apocalypse will be different. The process is a personal experience. Your ability and timing when predicting the initial outbreak can help you avoid the general populace's mass hysteria. Your psychological preparation can fortify your will to survive the horrors of the event. Your survival planning can eliminate the need for last minute reactive scrounging for resources and direction. Your actions can keep you out of trouble and on the right path to long term survival. Your proper medical training can keep an injury from reducing your health, or the health of others. Recognizing the importance of water and food, and knowing the sources of both in a zombie apocalyptic environment, can ensure your body receives the nutrients it needs to perform. Training with, and stockpiling, weapons for the occasions when you cannot avoid the aggressive corpses can save you from the undeadly infection and death. Knowing how to defensively move through zombie infested areas can enable you to get to and from necessary supplies, and to travel to areas of greater safety. Having a long term zombie survival retreat can give you the opportunity to live out the rest of your life in relative safety and security.

Enlist the cooperative efforts of others. Through synergy, with the right partners, the strength of your group will exceed the strength of its individuals. It is your duty to share your experience, skills, and resources with others. Your words of encouragement may be all a fellow prospective survivalist needs to make the lifestyle changes to prepare for the zombie apocalypse.

Strive for continuous improvement. No solution is perfect. In time, even one small improvement per day will reflect as significant overall improvement.

Rise to the responsibility of preparing yourself to survive the undead, beginning your journey today.

APPENDIX A – ADVANCE DIRECTIVE FOR AN UNNATURAL DEATH ("UNDEAD WILL")

ADVANCE DIRECTIVE FOR AN UNNATURAL DEATH ("UNDEAD WILL")

NOTE: YOU SHOULD USE THIS DOCUMENT TO GIVE YOUR FELLOW ZOMBIE SURVIVALISTS INSTRUCTIONS TO APPLY BRAIN DESTROYING MEASURES IN CERTAIN SITUATIONS. THERE IS NO LEGAL REQUIREMENT THAT ANYONE EXECUTE AN UNDEAD WILL.

GENERAL INSTRUCTIONS: *You can use this Advance Undead Directive ("Undead Will") form to give instructions for the future if you want your fellow zombie survivalists to apply brain destroying measures in certain situations. You should talk to your fellow zombie survivalists about what these terms mean. The Undead Will states what choices you would make for yourself if you were reanimated. Talk to your family members, friends, and others you trust about your choices. Also, it is a good idea to talk with professionals such as your doctors, clergypersons, and lawyers before you complete and sign this Undead Will.*

You do not have to use this form to give those instructions, but if you create your own Advance Undead Directive you need to be very careful to ensure that it is consistent with the spirit of the message.

This Undead Will form is intended to be valid in any zombie outbreak or apocalypse in which it is presented, but places outside your survival group's control may impose requirements that this form does not meet.

If you want to use this form, you must complete it, sign it, and have your signature witnessed by two qualified witnesses and proved by a notary public. Follow the instructions about which choices you can initial very carefully. **Do not sign this form until** *two witnesses and a notary public are present to watch you sign it. You then should consider giving a copy to your primary physician, every member in your zombie apocalypse preparedness home group, and a trusted relative.*

My Desire for an Unnatural Death

I, _____, being of sound mind, desire that, as specified below, my reanimation not be prolonged by zombifying measures:

1. **When My Undead Directives Apply**

My directions about prolonging my reanimation shall apply **IF** my fellow zombie survivalists determine that I lack capacity to make or communicate undead care decisions and:

NOTE: YOU MAY INITIAL ANY AND ALL OF THESE CHOICES.

_____
(Initial)

I have an infection that will result in my death and reanimation within a relatively short period of time.

_____
(Initial)

I become unconscious and my fellow zombie survivalists determine that, to a high degree of medical certainty, I will never regain my living human consciousness.

_____
(Initial)

I suffer from advanced zombism or any other condition which results in the substantial loss of my cognitive ability and motor skills, and makes me desire the ingestion of living flesh without concern to my personal health and safety and the health and safety of my fellow zombie survivalists.

2. These are My Directives about Prolonging My Reanimation:

In those situations I have initialed in Section 1, I direct that my fellow zombie survivalists:

NOTE: INITIAL ONLY IN ONE PLACE.

_____
(Initial)

may destroy my brain.

_____
(Initial)

shall destroy my brain.

3. Exceptions- "Excommunication or Confinement"

NOTE: INITIAL ONLY IF YOU WANT TO MAKE EXCEPTIONS TO YOUR INSTRUCTIONS IN PARAGRAPH 2.

EVEN THOUGH I do not want my reanimation prolonged in those situations I have initialed in Section 1:

_____
(Initial)
    I *DO* want to receive BOTH excommunication AND confinement measures (for example, being tied to a tree safely away from the group) in those situations.

_____
(Initial)
    I *DO* want to receive ONLY excommunication measures (for example, being released to fend for myself as a zombie ten miles away from the group) in those situations.

_____
(Initial)
    I *DO* want to receive ONLY confinement measures (for example, being locked in a room in the same vicinity as the group) in those situations.

4. I Wish to be Made as Comfortable as Possible

I direct that my fellow zombie survivalists take reasonable steps to keep me as clean, comfortable, and free of pain as possible so that my dignity is maintained, even though this care may hasten my death and reanimation.

5. I Understand my Advance Undead Directive

I am aware and understand that this document directs certain brain destroying measures to be enacted in accordance with my advance instructions.

6. If I have an Available Health Care Agent

If I have appointed a health care agent by executing a health care power of attorney or similar instrument, and that health care agent is acting and available and gives instructions that differ from this Advance Undead Directive, then I direct that:

> Follow Advance Undead Directive: This Advance Undead Directive will **override** instructions my health care agent give about prolonging my reanimation.

_____

(Initial)

> Follow Health Care Agent: My health care agent has authority to **override** this Advance Undead Directive.

_____

(Initial)

NOTE: DO NOT INITIAL BOTH BLOCKS. IF YOU DO NOT INITIAL EITHER BOX, THEN YOUR HEALTH CARE PROVIDERS WILL FOLLOW THIS ADVANCE DIRECTIVE AND IGNORE THE INSTRUCTIONS OF YOUR HEALTH CARE AGENT ABOUT PROLONGING YOUR REANIMATION.

7. My Fellow Zombie Survivalists May Rely on this Directive

My fellow zombie survivalists shall not be liable to me or to my family, my estate, my heirs, or my personal representative for following the instructions I give in this instrument. Following my directions shall not be considered suicide, or the cause of my death, or malpractice or unprofessional conduct. If I have revoked this instrument but my fellow zombie survivalists do not know that I have done so, and they follow the instructions in this instrument in good faith, they shall be entitled to the same protections to which they would have been entitled if the instrument had not been revoked.

8. I Want this Undead Directive to be Effective Anywhere

I intend that this Advance Undead Directive be followed by any fellow zombie survivalist in any place.

9. I have the Right to Revoke this Advance Undead Directive

I understand that at any time I may revoke this Advance Undead Directive in a writing I sign or by communicating in any clear and consistent manner my intent to revoke it to my fellow zombie survivalists.

I understand that if I revoke this instrument I should try to destroy all copies of it.

This the _____ day of _____, _____.

_____

APPENDIX B – GOAL SETTING

Zombie Preparedness is the state when the expectations of understanding the psychology of survival, planning to survive, putting that plan into action, applying survival medical procedures, finding water and food, defending yourself, successfully moving in zombie infested areas, and establishing a long term zombie apocalypse retreat, are met by your abilities.

Preparing yourself for the undead starts with a personal inventory of strengths and weakness, continues with setting goals, and culminates with continuous improvement.

Follow this goal setting exercise to identify your strengths and weaknesses, allowing you to better balance your preparedness, and develop the areas that you know are necessary to survive the undead.

Step 1. Using the 10 Chapters of Zombie Preparedness table, in the center column, make notes about what you find most frustrating in each chapter.

Step 2. Using the 10 Chapters of Zombie Preparedness table, in the right column, rate your skill level for each of the chapters. The scale ranges from 0 (worthless) through 5 (average) to 10 (master) with varying degrees of skill in-between.

Step 3. Using the Visual Wheel, translate your skill ratings to the dashes on each of the related lines. A rating of 5 would be the fifth dash from the center. A rating of 10 would be the dash furthest from the center.

Step 4. Draw a loop around the wheel connecting the rated dashes.

Step 5. Recognize out of balance areas by the loop's non-circular shape. Note your biggest revelation.

Step 6. To balance your zombie survival skills, write 2 goals per chapter on the Goals for Zombie Preparedness table. Goals should be SMART – Specific, Measurable, Attainable, Realistic, and Timely.

Step 7. Note your most important zombie preparedness goals. Start working to achieve them.

Step 8. Continuously improve your preparedness by repeating this exercise at the completion of each goal.

What frustrates you the most in preparing for the zombie apocalypse?

10 Chapters of Zombie Preparedness		Rate 1-10
Predicting Outbreaks		
Psychological Fortitude		
Survival Planning		
Survival Actions		
Medical		
Water Procurement		
Food Procurement		
Zombie Combat		
Survival Movement		
Long Term Survival Solutions		

JAMES C. SANDERS

Visual Wheel

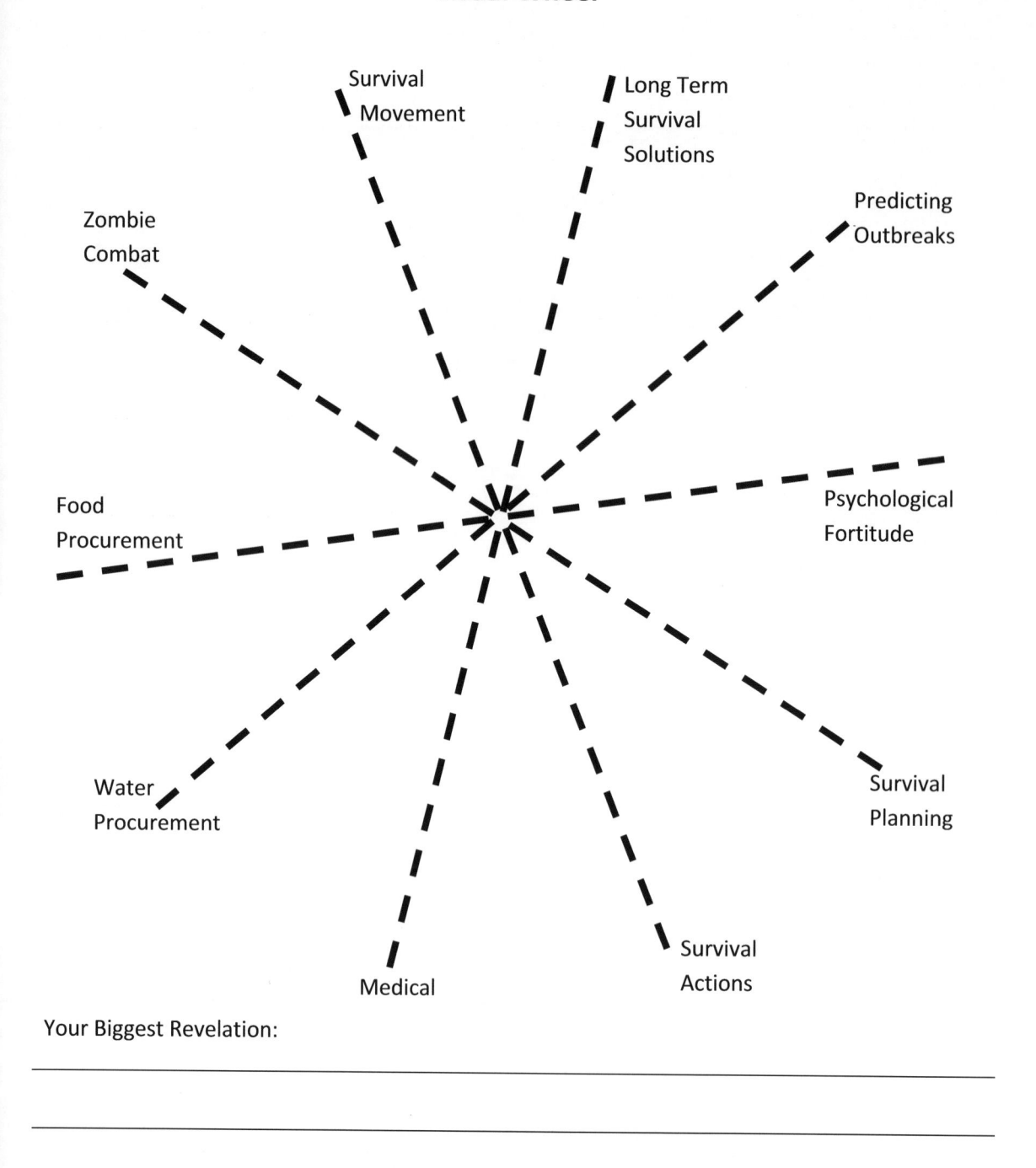

- Survival Movement
- Long Term Survival Solutions
- Predicting Outbreaks
- Zombie Combat
- Psychological Fortitude
- Food Procurement
- Survival Planning
- Water Procurement
- Medical
- Survival Actions

Your Biggest Revelation:

_____

_____

_____

ZOMBIE PREPAREDNESS VOLUME I

Goals for Zombie Preparedness

Predicting Outbreaks	1. 2.
Psychological Fortitude	1. 2.
Survival Planning	1. 2..
Survival Actions	1. 2.
Medical	1. 2.
Water Procurement	1. 2.
Food Procurement	1. 2.
Zombie Combat	1. 2.
Survival Movement	1. 2.
Long Term Survival Solutions	1. 2.

Your most important zombie preparedness goals:

_____

_____

_____

JAMES C. SANDERS

APPENDIX C - Adapted Standardized Hand Signals for Close Range Engagement

One	Two	Three	Four	Five
Six	Seven	Eight	Nine	Ten

You	Me	Zombie

ZOMBIE PREPAREDNESS VOLUME I

Come	Hurry Up	Stop
Listen or I Hear	Watch or I See	Freeze
Go Here or Move Up	Rally Point	Cover This Area

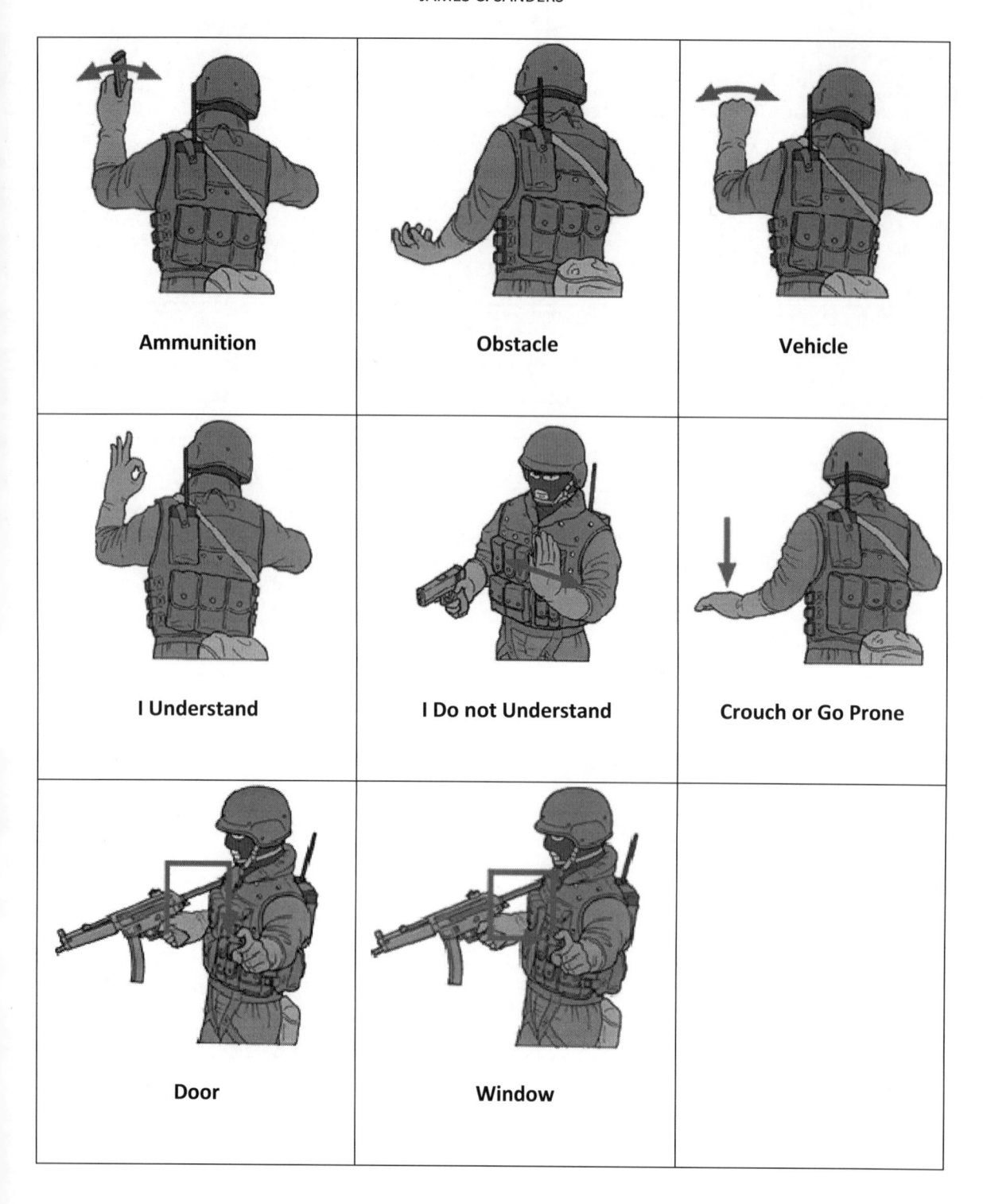

Ammunition	**Obstacle**	**Vehicle**
I Understand	**I Do not Understand**	**Crouch or Go Prone**
Door	**Window**	

ABOUT THE AUTHOR

James C. Sanders is an United States military veteran, Tennessee Squire, accomplished motorcyclist, and holds a Master of Business Administration in Information Technology Management from Western Governors University.

To fund his zombie preparedness, he proactively prevents computer downtime as Founder and President of a computer consulting firm in North Carolina.

James can be reached for discussion at
james@jamessanders.us

Printed in Great Britain
by Amazon.co.uk, Ltd.,
Marston Gate.